G000092517

HOW NOT TO MURDER YOUR GRUMPY

CAROL E WYER

DELANCEY PRESS
LONDON 2016

Published by Delancey Press Ltd
23 Berkeley Square
London W1J 6HE
www.delanceypress.co.uk

A CIP catalogue record for this title is available
from the British Library

This 3rd edition published 2016

Cover by Aimee Coveney –
www.authordesignstudio.com

Cover image by Small shrimp

Printed and bound in Great Britain by 4Edge Ltd.

ISBN   978-1-907205-38-5

e book: 978-1-907205-39-2

INTRODUCTION

If you have picked up this book, you more than likely have a Grumpy Old Man to deal with. You have my sympathy. Endearing as he might be, he'll need careful handling. If your Grumpy is suffering from "Irritable Male Syndrome", driving you mad by hanging around the house or facing retirement, then you have come to the right place.

You have here the key to the most difficult of achievements—keeping your GOM occupied, stimulated and most importantly, out from under your feet.

Take heart. There are over 700 ideas in this book to enchant your chap and entice him into a world of his own. They are not just your ordinary choices, selected randomly from a list. Many of the following activities and hobbies have been tested out on my very own retired Mr G. He has been the most perfect, unwitting guinea pig.

GOMs facing not just older age, but also retirement, will be anxious about their future. They will require challenges and activities to stimulate them. They have just spent their whole lives working and being occupied. Now they need other passions to keep them from feeling unworthy or depressed.

Recent research shows age is no barrier to pursuing hobbies:

- Nearly three quarters of Brits have tried new activities since turning 60.
- Fifty-three percent revel in the freedom that the later years offer.
- One in five Brits says active hobbies help them feel younger.

Many people over the age of 60 in the UK are embracing their senior years by taking up new activities, according to recent research from Age UK. Seventy-one percent of those are tackling new challenges like learning a foreign language, taking to the dance floor, or even getting the adrenaline pumping with outdoor activities like bungee jumping, kayaking, and mountain climbing.

There is no excuse for your grouch to stay at home and vegetate in his twilight years. He needs to stop wrestling with retirement and tackle a new venture, if only to prevent you from losing all patience and your own sanity.

In this book, you'll find a whole host of exciting ideas for your beloved Grumpy to try out. After all, a happy Grumpy is one less problem for you to deal with each day.

Author's note: No Grumpy Old Men were harmed in the writing of this book.

A

Without further ado, let's look at the abundance of activities that your Grumpy can enjoy beginning with the letter A.

Introduce your Grumpy to the absorbing and completely time-consuming hobby of aviation, particularly **aeroplanes**.

First, get him a copy of *Top Gun* (or any good film about flying) to whet his appetite. Next, purchase a trial flying lesson. He'll love it. Honestly, he will. Don't be mean though, and get him an aerobatic flight. He'll come home a horrible pasty shade of grey, and you'll never get him to agree to that holiday to Alicante you hoped you could take next year.

Once he has "the flying bug", ensure he signs up for flying lessons. Now, you'll have to make some serious economies to fund this new hobby, and you'll have to forget that holiday to Alicante for a while, but it'll be worth it. He'll soon transform into a new man, and which one of us wouldn't fancy a Tom Cruise-a-like coming home after a long day up in the clouds?

Flying doesn't just keep these Grumpy Old Men out of the house for an hour or two. Oh no, they have to get to the airfield early to set up, have a pre-flight briefing, a couple of cups of coffee and some cake, chat to their mates and ensure they have planned a route. Then, there is the actual flying, followed by a debrief, and the obligatory drink at the pub to recap the entire flight.

There are exams to be taken and much studying to be done. Many a night will be spent sitting at the dining table with pencils in their mouths, as they attempt to learn the principles of aviation law or meteorology. You'll be able to relax on the settee and watch all those soaps without any dark muttering coming from the other end.

You may find that you will need to learn the phonetic alphabet though, just to show willingness and give him a hand. Let me assist you by starting with: Golf, Romeo, Uniform, Mike, Papa, Yankee.

If you can't interest him in this particular hobby, then you could try him with a remote-controlled aircraft. This is the best of both worlds. He can fly his aeroplane without taking examinations, wherever he fancies, and it won't cost a fortune. There will be more about remote-controlled vehicles later.

Last but not least, you could offer him the chance to do some plane spotting. This is obviously the cheapest option, and can be enjoyed at the airport or in your back garden if you are fortunate enough to live under the flight path.

If he decides on the latter, you'll be able to book that trip to Alicante. After all, he'll see plenty of aeroplanes.

What do William Tell, Robin Hood, and Cupid have in common? The answer is **archery** or toxophily as it is also called. (You might need that piece of information for a pub quiz.)

Archery is one of the most ancient sports known to mankind. In ancient times and the medieval period, this activity was used for protecting people from enemies and for hunting wild animals. Today, it is regarded as a recreational activity or sport, and is looked upon as a way to improve concentration, mental strength, and precision ... where was I? Oh yes, sorry, I was thinking about Kevin Costner in the 1991 film *Robin Hood: Prince of Thieves* and got distracted. Today, two forms of archery are prevalent: target archery and field archery.

Sign your fractious man up for lessons and watch him improve, along with his game. Word of warning: don't let him place an apple on your head "for practice".

question: what did the lustful maiden
say to the handsome archer?
answer: you make me quiver.

There are an amazing number of activities beginning with the letter A, including **art, alpine skiing** (not much good if you live a long way from mountains), **angling, American football, allotments, anagrams, antiques, archaeology, arm wrestling, aromatherapy, arts and crafts, athletics,**

astronomy, astrology, astral projections, auctions, autographs, and **automobilia.**

Has your Grumpy still got a sense of adventure, like feisty Doris Long from Hayling Island, who threw herself from the top of the civic office building in Portsmouth on her 96th birthday, accompanied by BBC presenter Chris Evans and actor James Cordon, in a 220-foot **abseil?**
Doris, well known for her fund-raising efforts, has since broken her record of being the oldest person to abseil down a building, when she abseiled down a 200-foot block of flats on her ninety-seventh birthday. I wonder what plans she has for her next one.

Art comes in many forms and guises. I am a fan of works by Matisse, Jackson Pollack, and Picasso, so I don't know if I am the right person to guide you through the choices available for your man. There are books and materials galore for him to try out, and with luck, he will find what works best for him, be it charcoal or oil. If you can't find a medium that suits your grouchy fellow, hit him over the head with the easel.
Here are a few fun facts to hurl at him; see if you can capture his interest in this activity:

- Leonardo da Vinci worked on Mona Lisa for twelve to fifteen years intermittently.
- He also invented high heels. (Don't you just love this man?)
- Henri Matisse's painting Le Bateau spent forty-six days hanging upside down at the Museum of Modern Art in New York. No one noticed until then.
- English artist Andy Brown created a portrait of Queen Elizabeth II by stitching together 1,000 used tea bags.
- Picasso could draw before he could walk, and his first word was Spanish for pencil.
- The first pencil was invented in England in 1565. (I wonder if it was 2B or not 2B.)

QUESTION: WHAT DO YOU CALL AN AMERICAN DRAWING? ANSWER: A YANKEE DOODLE.

If you fail to bring out his artistic side, you could attempt to hook him with **angling**. And if you reel him in on this one, he'll be one of a staggering twenty percent of the population who have been freshwater fishing over the last ten years, according to a 2010 report in the *Angling Times*.

The report discovered that angling had become an acceptable pastime, even among the young. There was a thirty-five percent increase in rod licence sales over the decade, pointing to an increasing interest in this hobby.

I don't want to carp on about it, but if he fails to rise to this bait, a fish and chip supper will be the closest you'll get him to this hobby.

I was tempted to tell you about collecting **airline sick bags** as a hobby, but with the rise in budget airlines, it will soon be the case that you take your own.

Astronomy will probably be more to his taste than **astrology**. A dark starlit night and a large telescope can keep a GOM amused for some time. Ensure his lens is pointing in the direction of the stars and not towards next door's sixty-inch plasma screen television, even if they do have Sky and you don't.

I end this section with **amateur dramatics**. I am sure deep within your crotchety chap, there is a desire to express himself and be heard. There are many local amateur dramatic productions. If he can't act, he could get involved with the props, make-up, or costumes, filming the entire play, or serving ice creams in the intervals. "Surely, there must be something he can do, Lovey?"

B

Hobbies your other half might be encouraged to take up include the following: **birdwatching, butterflies, bowling** (forget Crown or lawn bowls—send him to France to learn the art of Boules), **bingo, badminton, battery-operated toys, bridge, bicycles,** or **bagpipes** (invest in a large stock of ear plugs if your man takes up the bagpipes).

More unusual hobbies might include **bungee jumping** from high structures such as bridges or specially made platforms while attached to a thick rubberised rope and harness. Think that might be too dangerous? Apparently not for John Macdonald of Eriskay, who dropped forty metres (131 feet) from the Garry Bridge in Killiecrankie, Perthshire, to mark his eightieth birthday in November 2011. However, he is not the oldest bungee jumper. The oldest recorded bungee jumper in the world is 96-year-old Mohr Keets, who jumped 216 metres (708 feet) off a bridge in South Africa in 2010.

If your Grumpy is still adventurous at heart but doesn't fancy launching himself off a bridge, you could encourage him to take up **bodyflying**, where he would be suspended in the air by means of jets of air blowing upwards from the ground.

When a skydiver jumps from a plane, their drop speed is around 120 miles per hour. In bodyflying, or indoor skydiving as it is sometimes called, air is blown upwards at a speed of 120 miles per hour which will lift a human body to simulate flying. This activity is undertaken indoors and the person flying can move his body up and down and do somersaults, rolls and many other manoeuvres.

There are a few places, Milton Keynes and Manchester for example, where you can send your GOM for this experience and, with a bit of luck, he'll come back not only exhilarated, but sporting a new hairstyle.

Not keen on the above? Why not drag him into the twenty-first century and introduce your sourpuss to the joys of **blogging**? This is a subject close to my heart, having started my own blog only a couple of years ago. I did it as an experiment and research for my novel *Mini Skirts and Laughter Lines*, in which a middle-aged woman sets up a blog to upload the blunders and bloopers that populate her days. Like the main character, I soon found myself part of an enormous supportive community of bloggers. Some of them are, in fact, Grumpy Old Men whose own blogs make me roar with laughter.

Your GOM could benefit hugely from starting up his own blog. There are a staggering number of bloggers in cyber-land, and although the majority appear to be female, statistics show that sixty percent of blogs in the States[1] are written by men.

Your Grumpy will like to moan or complain, and there can no better way to do it than online. He can vent about everything from the weather and finance to politics and the state of young people today, without unleashing it all onto you. He might even attract other Grumps, and they could form a grumpy online clan which should keep him out of mischief all day.

Blogs already run by grumpy guys include Grumpy Bloggers, Grumpy Git, and Grumpy Blog. See, he wouldn't be alone.

Blogs are easy to set up, cost nothing and fill oodles of time. The most popular blogging platforms are Wordpress and Blogger. Blogging started in the 1990s when people shared interests, hobbies, thoughts and so on. By 2012, it has become a major publishing business with blogs covering any subject. There are an estimated 31 million bloggers in the States.

You are never too old to blog, and indeed, some of my followers who also blog, are in their eighties. The world's oldest blogger, Ruth Hamilton, died three days shy of her 110th birthday. She blogged to the end.

If you fancy some muscle, then suggest he takes up **body building**. Don't let him tell you he is too old. Point him in the direction of 91-year-old Charles Eugster, who had a crisis at 85. According to an article in the *Guardian* (2011), "I looked at myself in the mirror and saw an old man. I was overweight, my posture was terrible and there was skin hanging off me. I looked like a wreck."

Since then, Charles has taken up body building, trains regularly and looks fantastic. He isn't chasing youth though; he is chasing health, and is a shining example to us all. If that doesn't serve to send him to the gym, pin up a photograph of a topless Sylvester Stallone training in the gym. He's 66 and will still make your heart flutter.

I should probably bounce over **breakdancing, belly dancing,** and **ballet** to mention **ballroom dancing.** I'll touch on this again under the letter D. I discovered various YouTube clips of aged people breakdancing, and one of a 90-year-old granny dancing to Whitney Houston. Even more impressive is Frederick Salter, who, after performing the rumba, cha-cha, samba, paso, waltz, quickstep, tango, and foxtrot, passed his IDTA Gold Bar Level 3 examinations in Latin and ballroom with honours at the age of 100 years 245 days, in Eltham, London, on 15th October 2011. He is the oldest competitive ballroom dancer in the world. (Information from *The Guinness World Records* 2013)

question: how do hens dance?
answer: chick to chick.

Akin to birdwatching is budgerigar-keeping. **Budgerigars** are believed to have been brought from Australia to England in 1840. In fact, bones discovered in Australia show that wild budgies have been on this planet even longer than humans. Budgies are the most popular pet in the world today and, with proper training, can learn to say about one hundred words. Unlike the human species, the males are more likely to talk or whistle than females. Don't let your Grumpy teach it, or it'll no doubt yell, "I can't believe it!" a hundred times a day.

Budgies might be chatterboxes, but **bees** are productive. Honey bees have been around for millions of years, and honey is the only food that includes all the substances necessary to sustain life, including enzymes, vitamins, minerals, and water. It also contains "pinocembrin", an antioxidant associated with improved brain functioning.

Bees are under threat at the moment, so your Grump would be doing us all a favour if he took up this hobby. Bees are generally very easy to keep, and if handled correctly, stings are rare. I would recommend he seeks professional advice, rather than buzzing off and starting up without correct guidelines.

question: what kind of bee hums and drops things?
answer: a fumble bee.

question: what kind of bee can't be understood?
answer: a mumble bee.

question: who is a bee's favourite painter?
answer: pablo beecasso.

question: what do bees do if they want to use public transport?
answer: wait at a buzz stop.

Okay, I'll stop now and move onto my next suggestion, which should hold a certain appeal: **Beer**. Not just the drinking of beer, as enjoyable as that may seem, or brewing of beer, which you can read about under Home Brew, but the collection of beer caps, tops, glasses, bottles, or mats. You can take the last one a little further and attempt beer-mat flipping. It'll take some time before your Grumpy will be able to beat a record set by Mat Hand, who flipped and caught a pile of 112 beer mats in 2001 in Nottingham, UK. It took him over 4 hours and 129 attempts before he broke the previous record of 111. (Information from The Guinness World Records 2012)

Other activities include **billiards, books, brass rubbing, brass bands, botany, bonsai, bus tickets**, and last but not least, **bus racing**, which is probably best tried out in game form, even though the BBC programme *Top Gear* attempted to bring it to life. Genuine races are held in the States, but I found little evidence of any in the UK. I can't see it catching on here, somehow.

C

The list of hobbies beginning with the letter C offers a cornucopia of delights. Possibilities include: **caravans, canal boats, coin-collecting** (they should be good at that since they don't like spending money), **cooking, calligraphy, crossword puzzles, clay pigeon shooting, CAMRA** (real-ale drinking), **cinema, cribbage, cricket, curtain-making,** or **crocheting.**

The melodic sound of church bells ringing on a Sunday morning could mean more than a welcome to church. It could mean your GOM is out of the house practising his new hobby of **campanology**. It is quite an art, and some musical knowledge is required, but if you could pique his interest, not only will he be out of the house on a Sunday morning, allowing you to have a peaceful lie-in, but he'll need to go to bell-ringing practice. These often occur on an evening, which will mean you can watch your favourite soaps on television—the ones he invariably complains about. "Dingdong … result!"

Doesn't ring his bell? Given that any old Grumpy harps on about the *Good Old Days*, especially where **cars** are concerned, why not invest in a project for him? Encourage him to buy an old car, one with a "proper" engine he can work on, that will require hours of labour and much mess in your kitchen, but will keep your beloved a happy man. A few days working on an old car and bringing it back to life will put a smile on any crabby face.

To make sure this is a project for him, start by questioning him about his first car. If he gets all misty-eyed about that Mini he used to own, then you know you have cracked it. Check through motoring magazines for a cheap second-hand car, and Bob's your uncle. Give it to him tied up with a large bow as a present with the heart-felt message, "I thought you would like to recapture the nostalgia of the good old days." Chances are he'll find it quite appealing, immediately recalling the days when he spent weekends tinkering with his car. Do your research and find a members' club for him to join. too. He'll need all the support and help he can get when he can't fix the wretched thing or source an out-of-date spark plug for it.

Many couples decide to buy a **camper van** and travel when they retire. This may be a good idea if you are quite happy to spend every second of every minute of every day of every week with your Grumpy. Be warned. You'll soon tire of scenery, eating from picnic plates and sitting beside Mr Grumpy as he complains about the 'idiot drivers' abroad. Remember you won't be able to escape from his complaints.

One way to send him off to explore the scenery, without you having to tag along, is to buy him a bike. (Not a tandem!) There are many **cycling** clubs he could join, and if he gets good enough at it, he'll be able to participate in races. Who knows, you might be able to pack him off to the Tour de France in no time, either to watch or to participate.

Cycling is very addictive, and I know lots of middle-aged men who cycle most of the day or over the whole weekend. Sadly, my own Grumpy is not one of them. Two weeks after getting his bike, he decided he didn't like the saddle, the busy roads, and being covered in mud all the time.

If your GOM pooh-poohs this idea, stating he's too old to cycle, tell him about Octavio Orduno, who continued to cycle at the grand old age of 103. The Long Beach resident was declared the world's oldest cyclist in 2011. Born the same year the Ford Motor Company began production on the Model T, which revolutionised the automobile world, Octavio preferred to cycle, and even after he reached the age of one hundred, continued to ride around his neighbourhood on his bike.

Equally, you can bring out the Boy Scout in him and send him off **camping**. I bet he grumbles about modern life, and how the simplicity of the countryside and living frugally is the way to go. Here's your chance. Rummage about for that old tent you haven't used since 1970, and send him off to 'find himself'. He'll be able to get back to nature, cook beans on a camp fire, and sing *Ging Gang Goolie*. Camping is a great option for those men who want to get away from the madness of the modern world. Don't give in and let him take a hot-water bottle for those cold nights.

If you can't get him excited about any of the above, what about practising the art of **cheese rolling**? He could go to a nearby hill, start with a small Babybel cheese and progress to larger round cheeses. Cheese rolling is thought to date back to the 19th century, but could even be from Pagan times. The annual cheese rolling contest is held at Coopers Hill, Gloucestershire. Contestants run down a near vertical hill chasing after a round of cheese. The winner's prize is a twenty-five pound hunk of Double Gloucestershire cheese. Think of all the cheese sandwiches or cauliflower cheese dishes you could make with that.

A less gruelling and indeed less dangerous hobby is **cloud spotting**. That should keep him occupied, at least in the UK. He could seek out interesting cumulus or cirrus cloud formations, or take up general cloud spotting, which has been an interesting art form for many centuries. Cloud spotters try to find and photograph cloud shapes that resemble other objects such as animals or faces etc. Only the other day, I saw a cloud that looked like a hippopotamus playing a trombone. I'm sure I would be good at this hobby. There are cloud-spotter manuals and websites for him to check out, and in the UK, there is even a Cloud Appreciation Society.

question: what do you call a sheep
with no legs?
answer: a cloud.

You could, of course, introduce him to **cookery**. After several decades of cooking for the family, letting Grumpy become the next Heston Blumenthal has a certain appeal. Men relish being in charge at barbecues, so why not let them loose in the kitchen full-time? At least that way they wouldn't complain when dinner is late, cold, or burnt.

Should he show a flair for cookery, move him onto **cake decoration**. Tempt him with suggestions of producing a cake that looks like a beer bottle, or one in the shape of a television. In reality, he is far more likely to enjoy eating cake, rather than icing it.

He might be more amused by the hobby of **candle making**. He would appreciate being able to turn leftover wax from (expensive) used candles into reusable ones, thus saving money. The danger is that this idea will blossom into something meaningful as your GOM seeks out other ways to save money and reuse leftovers. Candles and soap are only the beginning.

I suppose a better option is **computer games**, which can keep him busy for hours. Though there could be a problem if, like my own Grumpy, yours hates new technology and is baffled by why people would spend hours shooting fat birds through the air.

There is an abundance of choice then for activities beginning with the letter C. Still not settled on one? My final offering will allow you both to relax, enjoy some sun and eat plenty. Buy him a sailor's hat and book a **cruise**. Bon voyage!

D

Your disgruntled other half might dabble with some of these options: **decorating eggs, darts, dinky toys, dingy sailing, dominos, drawing**, or **draughts** (the game variety, rather than standing in front of windy doors).

There are other more unusual hobbies and slightly daft ideas, such as **deep-sea diving**, which requires skill and fitness, or **dragon boat racing** (you might have to send your Grumpy to China to take up the latter). I'll talk about scuba diving at a later stage, but I had to mention **diving** here, purely so I could bring up the name of Jason Stratham, who was a champion diver before he became a famous actor. It gave me the chance to have a few lustful moments while researching this chapter.

I also discovered a YouTube interview with an astonishingly youthful 83-year-old man, Tom Hairabedian, who attributes his looks and health to eating a diet of raw food and diving. This hobby will require stamina, and a certain gymnastic grace. Somehow, I can't envisage other swimmers being delighted at the prospect of your Grump bombing them in the water.

I might be wrong, but I think you would have difficulty in getting him interested in **decoupage, dressmaking**, and **dried-flower arranging**. Still, you should never say never. Imagine the advantages of having a man who can whip up a super outfit for your Friday night out with the girls, or ensure the table decorations look impressive when friends pop around.

Onto more viable options now. What about **dancing?** Frankly, if your man is happy to take up dancing, then you shouldn't need to read any more of this book. Drag your little black number or your disco outfit out of hibernation, and hit the town with him.

Many men (like mine) only dance after several drinks, when they are forced into it by their partners. They then manage to do the universal penguin dance, where they shuffle about uncomfortably on the dance floor, arms clamped to their sides (also like mine).

If, however you have a budding John Travolta on your hands, then watch out when you send him to dance classes—he'll suddenly become extremely desirable. Every woman at the class will want to dance with your man, rather than their female friend who accompanied them to the classes. You don't want him getting too comfortable trotting the light fantastic with sequined Dolly from Essex, do you?

No joy with the dancing option? Try encouraging your Grumpy to get involved in an ancient art that dates back to the Egyptian times: the art of making salt dough and **dough craft**. It's a bit like playing with grown-up Play-Doh. In many past cultures, this art was closely linked to religious beliefs and ceremonies, when sculptures would have been offered as gifts to the gods or important people on special occasions like weddings.

It's easy enough to make the salt dough. You add one cup of table salt to two cups of plain flour and a cup of lukewarm water. Mix all the ingredients into a fairly stiff dough and roll it out. Add colouring, and leave to dry out in the air or the oven.

When it is ready, spray it with paint or varnish. At Christmas, he can make lots of decorations for the house. These will cost next to nothing, thus making him happy at a time of the year where ordinarily, he is a bigger grouch than normal.

There are alternatives for this absorbing hobby, like *Fimo*, which is similar but comes ready prepared, or indeed Plasticine, which has enjoyed a revival having been used in the *Wallace and Gromit* clay animation films, and after James May and over 2,000 members of the public created a show garden for the Chelsea Flower Show in 2009. See, there is nothing childish about this hobby.

Something meatier that might appeal to his appetite is **drag racing**. Tickle his palate or indeed impress him with this brief history:

The sport of drag racing originated in California, USA, after the Second World War, when people souped-up older pre-war cars with bigger and more powerful engines. It was not unusual to find these enhanced, more powerful cars side-by-side at traffic lights, attempting to out-accelerate when the light turned to green. The authorities soon realised they couldn't control this sport, and so started providing waste ground on which these cars could race each other—drag strips. In the mid-1960s, drag racing started to appear in the UK, when Sidney Allard brought over a team of American cars and drivers to race each other at various drag festivals around the country.

Soon, British cars and drivers were taking on the Americans, and the sport has now spread across the world. There are many racing circuits in the UK that have these events, including the popular Santa Pod Raceway in Wellingborough, Northamptonshire, which is host to the televised FIA European Drag Racing Championships and many other events all year round.

Surely this will bring back the boy racer in him. Still not hooked him? Get him a chilled beer and sit him down in front of one of these films:

- *Rebel Without a Cause.* This famous movie starring James Dean has a noteworthy drag racing scene.
- *American Graffiti.* This 1950's nostalgia-inspiring film includes a race on Paradise Road. There is even an explosion at the end of the scene. It doesn't get any more exciting than that.
- *The Fast and the Furious.* An undercover cop tries to infiltrate the underground street racing scene in Los Angeles. There is plenty of great drag racing to watch.

I could also suggest **drifting** to you at this point. This is sometimes known as power drifting and is a very popular motor sport in Japan. Cars are specially modified to allow the drivers to perform slides or spins around bends. The sport came to the UK in 2006. I have reservations about this, though. After I suggested it to my man, we spent half an hour attempting to drift round a large vacant roundabout until I felt rather sick.

More gentle but absorbing hobbies include the game **Dungeons & Dragons**, also known as D&D, which is a fantasy role-playing game designed by Gary Gygax and David Arneson in the early 1970s. Incredibly popular, even today, it can be played by old and young alike. If your man suddenly has the urge to walk around in a wizard hat, don't question it. He's obviously getting into character.

D is for **drawing**. Many local villages and towns offer art classes. Pencils and paper are not expensive, and if he becomes proficient, you'll have endless artwork to give as Christmas presents or decorate your walls with. Careful you don't send him to a live art class. One friend sent her husband to an art class that used a male model. Her husband broke his charcoal stick in anxiety after the male model winked at him and blew him a kiss.

The letter D is also for the most popular hobby of all: **DIY**. Do It Yourself can take up all of your Grumpy's free time, and probably all of your own patience. If your man is anything like mine, he will require assistance at all times as he sets about improving your nest, which looked perfectly fine for decades, until he retired. I have been known to stand for hours holding screws, bolts, bits of plastic, shelves and so on while he sorts out where he is going to put them.

Once involved in a project, your Grumpy will require encouragement and enthusiasm. He might want to take you out to the local DIY store to shop for some bits and pieces. DIY shopping for women is what clothes shopping is for men; it is dull. How a man can get excited about row upon row of hinges or glues is beyond me.

You will also have to put up with noise, mess, muttering, and occasional swearing as projects don't go to plan. You may find your Grumpy is able to transform your home with his hard labour, but DIY is best taken up if you have offspring who will welcome Dad's help. You can pack him off to their house, thus leaving you to get on in peace.

E

Electronics, engraving, early medieval historical re-enactments, English civil war enactments, e-Bay trading, enamelling; the letter E offers endless possibilities in terms of entertainment.

Exercise is an obvious choice. There are so many possibilities in that category, I can't begin to list them all here. There is no doubt your grumbling other half would benefit from some form of exercise, be it walking, or one of those listed under unusual hobbies.

It has been proven that regular exercise is not only beneficial to your physical health but, thanks to the release of endorphins, also good for your mental health, promoting a feeling of well-being. Send him out for a ten-mile walk, and he should come home in a decent mood, or just too exhausted to whinge.

One word of caution at this stage; if Grumpy begins to notice an improvement in his health and shape, he'll more than likely suggest that you join him and take it up. It all depends on how good you think you'll look in lycra.

"my granddad started walking five miles a day when he reached 60. now he's 97 years old and we don't know where the heck he is."

"the only reason i would take up walking is so i could hear heavy breathing again."

"I have to walk early in the morning, before my brain figures out what I am doing."

Should he not be smitten by the exercise bug, then you could introduce him to this craze: **Eddie Stobart** spotting. Thanks to the Channel 5 television documentary *Eddie Stobart—Trucks and Trailers*, there are now thousands of fans who hang out by the sides of the road, attempting to spot a truck and write down the name emblazoned on the front.

Over 6,500 members and fans came from all over the country to attend the first ever Eddie Stobart Festival. As of August 2012, there were 2,280 trucks and 3,500 trailers. So there is ample opportunity to spot a truck and note its name.

Send your curmudgeon out to stand by the local dual carriageway, thermos in one hand and new jotting pad in the other. Added bonus: he might like it so much, he decides to become a full-time trucker.

If your grouchy man likes to shake his hips and say "Uh huh!" save up and take him to the home of the King in Graceland, Memphis, Tennessee. You might even get him interested in collecting **Elvis** memorabilia. In time, it could be worth a bit for your great-great-great grandchildren.

There is, of course, an official fan club for Elvis in the UK that he could join, as well as a large number of Elvis tribute acts. There are, in fact, more Elvis impersonators around the world than for any other performer. Buy him some stick-on sideburns, teach him the lyrics to *Jailhouse Rock*, and send him out on his own tour. Just keep your fingers crossed he doesn't attract too many groupies.

Would your Grumpy fancy becoming part of the large group of people who are interested in **equestrian** activities? There are a number of ways he could be involved. He should begin by taking up riding lessons at your local stables, although he will stand out among the five-year-olds learning to control a pony.

He might, however, be more interested in the racing and betting side of it. A day at the races can be very entertaining, particularly if you can hide out in the champagne tent while Mr Grumpy gets to grips with the form of the horses.

It isn't just about racing though. Equestrian sports are numerous and varied. Cross-country, dressage, endurance, eventing, hunting, show jumping, vaulting, hacking, and point-to-point are activities you can observe or even enjoy mounted on a horse. I quite fancy horseball. There'll be more on that subject later in the book. Polo is also a popular activity but how about trying elephant polo? It would mean sending your man to Nepal, Sri Lanka, or Thailand. That isn't a problem, is it?

Less demanding activities include collecting and rereading Enid Blyton books. My own hubby still has his childhood collection—all of Enid Blyton's works. Ordinary first editions can range from £30 to £140, although a first edition of *The Island of Adventure* owned by Enid Blyton in its original crimson wrapper is available for purchase for £2,750. I must check through hubby's collection sometime.

Although you would not think this next pastime would apply to men, you should run it past your GOM. Give him these facts first, though, so he knows you are being serious. **Embroidery** as a profession was practised by both men and women during the middle ages. It was mostly classified as a woman's hobby after that period, and rejected by men, with the exception of sailors. All sailors were skilled stitchers—after all, every time a sail ripped, they couldn't just pull into shore to get it repaired.

Over time, they experimented with decoration and began to use the same stitches they used to mend sails to decorate clothing using coloured thread.

During the First World War, embroidery classes, run by the Red Cross, were given to men as part of rehabilitation for wounds and shell shock. These classes were revived with the advent of World War II, and for many it remained a hobby.

More recently, with the emergence of historical re-enactment as a popular hobby, there are more amateur male embroiderers. In England, one of the best-known male embroiderers is Leon Conrad, whose speciality is Blackwork.

Now, find all those holey socks, and let your cranky man get stitching.

Entomology or studying insects is not really a hobby I would like my own Grump to take up. If you are less squeamish than I, and can put up with dissected beetles adorning your tables, then be my guest and encourage your other half to start his own collection. Excuse me while I shudder at the thought.

The next few ideas intrigued me so much I had to introduce them to you: **extreme ironing, extreme kayaking,** and **extreme tree climbing**. I must point out here and now that they are, in my opinion, accidents waiting to happen.

Extreme ironing is a dangerous sport which, according to the official website, "combines the thrills of an extreme outdoor activity with the satisfaction of a well-pressed shirt". The idea is to see who can iron in the most bizarre, unusual or extreme place. Photographs have been taken of contestants ironing on top of mountains, in the middle of the M1 motorway, in fast-flowing rivers, on top of moving cars, suspended from trees, and even at the bottom of the sea.

Purists believe the sport was invented by Phil 'Steam' Shaw from Leicester one day in 1997, as he walked home from work at the local knitting factory. The idea took off, and the first Extreme Ironing World Championship was held in 2002 in a small town outside of Munich, Germany. Great Britain won.

Earlier this year, a super-fit runner established a new distance record for running with an ironing board on his back, by completing the 155-mile Marathon Des Sables in the Sahara Desert. Now that brings a whole new meaning to getting a sharp crease in your trousers!

So, tie your ironing board to the top of a step ladder, and let Mr G get some practice in on the weekly wash. You might kill two birds with one stone, or ironing board.

There are other extreme sports like **extreme cello playing, extreme caravan towing, extreme cliff and mountain top skydiving,** and **extreme wheelbarrow pushing**, which is believed to have originated on a building site in London. *Disclaimer—I take no responsibility for any accident that may occur should your Grumpy attempt to take up these ridiculously dangerous sports.

Your Grump may be bored, but surely he isn't bonkers enough to try these, is he?

F

Finding hobbies beginning with the letter F is fascinating. There are a formidable number to choose from. I'll begin with these: **fishing, film watching, fencing** (not the one where you put up wooden posts, the one where you stab people with sharp swords, or épées, to be more correct), **falconry, fire walking, freestyle skiing, freestyle wrestling, Feng Shui, free diving, frisbee throwing, free running, fast food restaurants, fossils, ferry crossing.**

First Aid isn't so much a hobby as a necessity if your grump decides to embark upon frightful activities like fencing, fire eating, and freestyle wrestling. It sneaks in as an activity or hobby because you can send your man on courses. First aid information is useful, and we could all benefit by learning more.

As a taster, here are some things you thought you should do but you shouldn't do—if that makes sense:

- Don't put a steak on a black eye. Frozen peas are better. Ensure they stay in the bag. It won't work if you use them pea by pea.
- Never pull a bee stinger out. You might leave the sac and venom behind. Use a credit card to scrape it all out. I heard they'll even take American Express. You could also try putting baking soda on the infected area. If the person goes red or has trouble breathing, then dial the emergency services.
- Peeing on a jelly fish sting will only get you strange looks from others. It will not relieve the pain (only your bladder). You should use vinegar. Having said this, I know people who say urine does help!
- Don't tilt your head back if you have a nose bleed. You should lean forward and press the fleshy part of your nose hard as if trying to stop a bad smell. You must do this for a good ten minutes. Ten whole minutes, people. Don't keep checking every three or four.

Obviously, I have only touched on this subject, and if you would like to know more, then make sure you get the correct advice, and/or go on a course.

When Googled, "flower arranging for men" only offers a few suggestions. I expect that comes as no surprise. It is, after all, a hobby normally undertaken by women. **Flower arranging** is creative, and if your Grumpy can be cajoled into having a go, he might be pleased with the results. On the other hand, he'll probably decide to leave it to you and go down to the pub to hide.

Out of all the hobbies available beginning with the letter F, your crotchety man should be naturally programmed for **finances**. As men become older, they seem to have even less desire than normal to part with their hard-earned cash. They are even worse if they are drawing a pension. Should your Grumpy get involved in the world of finance, be that an interest in shares, the global economy, or just how much you spend a month at the hairdresser's, then be prepared not only for incessant grumblings about falling share prices and depressed GAD rates, but also sharp changes to your lifestyle.

Your curmudgeon will no doubt decide to chart monthly household expenditure and take hold of the purse strings. If you are very unlucky, like me, you will be presented each month with a spreadsheet of just how much has been spent on fuel, food, clothes, and going out. The heating will immediately be turned down or off. Every penny you spend will be scrutinised, and he will begin to take an unhealthy interest in how much you spend on cosmetics, clothes, and other "little purchases" that, up until now, have passed under his radar.

He will offer sage advice on how you should cut out the coupon he saw in the local free newspaper, entitling you to a twenty percent saving on your next shop. Worse still, he'll accompany you to the supermarket, where he will insist on buying only the reduced items, leaving you to fathom out how to make supper using only a half-priced grapefruit, six boxes of porridge, and some reduced cans of Spam that are dangerously close to their sell-by date.

Your personal expenditure will come under attack too, and you might even find he suggests that you grow your hair long and that natural grey is the way forward. You will have to be prepared to be ultra-sneaky, if you still want to get that copy of the magazine you usually buy and read at the nail salon. If he seems tempted by this hobby, take his mind off it immediately!

A safe bet is to let him get completely involved in **football**. What could be better than a man who watches all the football matches on television, who goes out to watch his side play, who plays or coaches the local village team, and who is often to be found at the pub with his mates rather than making rude comments about the romantic comedy you want to watch on BBC2? Well, it's the next best thing to golf in my book, although, on the downside, you have to put up with them hogging the television set and yelling at the screen when their side does badly.

If he is not a football fanatic and prefers a more stimulating hobby, try him on **furniture restoration**. I bet that sofa you have had for twenty years could do with being reupholstered, or the pine table your children bashed to death in their youth could do with a French polish. Send your Grumpy on a course at the local education centre and you can leave him working happily on an old piece of furniture, while you nip out to spend the money you would have wasted on a new piece of furniture on something more useful, like a new pair of shoes.

Other hobbies or interests I am not keen on, but might appeal to you and your man are **ferret keeping**, collecting **fossils** (I have one of those—called "Hubby"), and **fire eating**. I don't mind if my GOM wants to have a go at fire eating, but I think I should up the insurance on the house in case he sets fire to the curtains.

Farm tractors and machinery tends to appeal to a lot of men, particularly as they get older. A proper John Deere tractor is out of the question, due to its price, and the fact it won't sit on the front drive very easily, but you could let him collect models or tinker with an old lawn mower or equivalent. Just don't let him do it on your kitchen table, or you'll be the one taking up furniture renovation.

Flash your man's black stretchy trousers, white shirt with short black jacket and shiny shoes at the local dance when he has finished his lessons in **Flamenco**.

Flamenco is the dance of the gypsies, conjuring up images of passion and vibrancy. Another word for gypsies is "flemenc". These gypsies migrated to Spain from Turkey, and, as their culture interacted with that of the Moors and other cultures, Flamenco developed.

True Flamenco dancers do not choreograph; there is no proper routine. The gypsy simply listens to the music, rises dramatically when led to do so, and then begins finding her own song with the tapping of her feet. From then on, it is the guitarist's job to follow the lead of the dancer.

The male dancer must interact with the female in this heavily practised dance, but I suggest you get your man to become a solo performer. We don't want to bring out too much passion in the old chap.

Rather than tell you about the oldest male Flamenco dancer in the world, I thought I'd bring El Willy the Chihuahua to your attention. You can find a cute video of this little dog doing the Flamenco on YouTube. He might be even better at it than your GOM.

G

question: how many golf players does it take to change a light bulb? answer: fore!

I wish I were a **golf** widow. I would love to have long days to myself while Mr G plays eighteen holes, then spends the evening at the nineteenth. Sadly, Mr G hates golf. He took it up some time ago, and we bought him the obligatory kit: shoes, one white glove, clubs, club bag, furry animal covers for clubs, loud checked trousers, jumper to match, and a set of fifty very expensive brightly coloured balls. We were assured that they would be very difficult to lose, and since Grumpy was a novice, he would inevitably spend the first few lessons digging his balls out of bunkers and undergrowth. Being luminous yellow, red and orange, these balls would be easy to spot.

After several lessons on the driving range, Grumpy set off to play his first game with a friend. I have a lasting image of the two of them packed into a golf buggy; the scene reminded me of Fred Flintstone and Barney Rubble leaving work together in the cartoon *The Flintstones*. I could almost hear them shout "Yabba, dabba doo!" They zoomed off at high speed. Several hours later he returned, grim-faced. He had lost every single ball. They had all landed in the large expanse of water in the middle of the course never to be seen again.

Golf is the most popular sport for retired men and women. Once only available to club members, it is now accessible to everyone in the UK, with over 3,000 golf courses. Of course, should you decide to take it up too, you could enjoy your twilight years together playing on courses not just in the UK, but all over the world. Tempting, isn't it?

If you have already got a Grump who is interested in golf, impress him with these facts: the first golf balls used in the 16th century are believed to have been made out of wood; feather balls, made of thin leather and stuffed with feathers, were used until 1848—tightly packed feathers made balls that flew the farthest; the number of dimples on a golf ball is either 336 for an American ball or 330 for a British ball; the word 'caddy' comes from the French word for student—cadet—which is pronounced cad-day; 125,000 golf balls a year are hit into the water at the famous 17th hole of the Stadium Course at Sawgrass, Florida, USA; the highest golf course in the world is the Tactu Golf Club in Morococha, Peru, which sits 14,335 feet above sea level at its lowest point.[2]

Enough about golf. Alternatives, then, for Grumpy Old Men like mine, whose golf clubs recently went to a charity shop, include **glass blowing**, **greyhound racing**, **guitar lessons**, and **gramophone records**.

Your other half probably has a large collection of gramophone records because he has refused to move with the times and buy CDs, believing that record players would make a comeback. He was right—they have! You can now buy record players again, so ensure he has his old 33 rpm albums, from those days when Bing Crosby was a newly discovered sensation.

Another extremely popular pastime is **gardening**. I don't need to say much about this, especially as I loathe weeding, but I would like to add that there are many men, who are interested, not just in gardening, but in garden sheds.

Garden sheds are actually classified as a hobby or interest. Don't ask me what they get up to in their sheds, but anything that keeps them out of the house is a bonus, so check out wooden sheds at local garden centres and suggest he gets one. Buy him a travel kettle, some plastic plates and mugs along with a small fridge for beer, and you stand a chance of him spending quite a bit of time out there. If you can get a television fitted and a sofa in there, you have cracked it.

---

2   *Golf facts – Source http://www.intotherough.co.uk/golf-features/20-facts-you-didn-t-know-about-golf/*

Genealogy has become increasingly popular, thanks to television programmes such as *Who Do You Think You Are?* Researching has become easier due to the internet, but you can't beat tracking down records at official offices or church archives. Suggesting that your GOM tracks down his ancestors could lead to some fascinating results; after all, he might have to travel abroad to seek out some distant relative, and that could turn into a holiday for you, too.

All of this brings me nicely onto my favourite hobby in this category: a **gap year**.

Each year, more than 100,000 travellers set off from the UK on an exotic adventure, which may last anything from one month to a year. Although the majority are students taking a break between school and college or university, a growing number of seniors is embracing gap-year ideology.

Having not had the chance to travel the world when they were younger, as package holidays were not invented until the 1960s, these people are looking to try new experiences, such as helping to save turtles in the Seychelles, or work on projects in countries where people are less fortunate than us.

Should your finances not stretch to a Grey Gap Year, then you can always take huge pleasure from this interest beginning with the letter G: being a **grandparent**. When your children need a babysitter, you know who they'll ask first, and who cannot resist being with their grandchildren for the day? They'll keep you on your toes and young at heart.

Not getting excited by these choices? My next offering could grip you: **games**. Board games have always been incredibly popular, and are particularly good in helping with memory. Favourites include: Scrabble, Chess, Backgammon, Chinese Checkers, Parcheesi, Mah Jongg. Okay, I didn't know what the last three were, and had to ask my elderly neighbours, who play board games daily.

Chinese Checkers is a basic and simple game, which involves some logic and sequencing. It provides hours of mental stimulation. Parcheesi, which also goes by the names "Trouble" and "Sorry", is less technical and involves simple dice and counters to move around a board. Traditional Mah Jongg is played with tiles and can be a long game with multiple players. Board games usually involve at least two players, so, unless you want to be your Grumpy's play friend, it would be an idea to get him to join clubs where other enthusiasts play. That way, he'll meet new people, and you won't have to let him win so he doesn't sulk all afternoon.

If flying lessons are out of your budget, you can achieve similar results by sending him **gliding**. I bought my "impatient one" a gliding lesson for a birthday present. We rolled up at the appointed time of ten o'clock only to be told the weather wasn't suitable, so we could stay and join the band of volunteers who were going to clean out the gutters around the hangar, or come back another day. We returned the following week when the skies finally cleared.

We were treated to a plastic chair each, and sat with twenty members in the hangar to listen to the briefing on jobs for the day. Each member was assigned a task. Some were on the radio;

others were offered the opportunity to drive the glider recovery vehicles, cutely named Bill and Ben. Six excited members jostled for that job, which led us to believe gliding wasn't too much fun. We all helped remove the gliders from the hangars and carted them outside.

Mr G waited five hours before he was able to get his flight, because one member had gone up ahead of him and, having caught some great thermals, had remained airborne for much longer than he should have. The members were clearly used to this and were sitting about in the sunshine, eating sandwiches from plastic containers and doing crossword puzzles.

Eventually, the old soul was harnessed into his glider. I watched as he was propelled with alarming alacrity, from what I can only describe as a giant rubber band, into the azure blue sky. He completed one circuit, having failed to find a thermal, and headed straight back down. He was offered another chance but declined it, preferring to watch the men who had grabbed the job of collecting the gliders and who were now enjoying themselves racing each other on the airstrip in their machines.

Our experience was not the norm, it has to be said, and gliding is a hobby that attracts many retired people. Check out hang-gliding, paragliding and parasailing for more information.

Other activities like **go-karting** or **grass boarding** (known also as mountainboarding, dirtboarding, and offroadboarding; it is like snowboarding, but on grass) could hold appeal for an adrenaline-seeking Grumpy. He'll need a helmet and protective knee pads, and you'll probably need to take out life insurance in case of accidents.

H is for **hip hop dancing** (although as Harry Enfield and Paul Whitehouse said in one of their sketch shows, "we are probably more hip op than hip hop"), **horror films, homing pigeons, horse riding, hunting,** and **housework**. Eureka! Now there's a super activity for your Grumpy. He would look fetching in a pinafore (think Queen's Freddy Mercury in the *I Want to Break Free* video), and he wouldn't be able to complain at how you've missed a cobweb ever again.

A fit and active misery guts could try **hiking** or **hill walking**. It'll keep him in good shape, and, if you live in Norfolk, will involve a very long drive before he finds any suitable slopes to walk up, resulting in him being out all day.

There are numerous organisations for hill walkers, ramblers, and walking groups. Just Google "hill walking" and you'll find lots of useful information. Stock up on a decent supply of Kendall Mint Cake for those arduous walks where he'll need sustenance.

If he is more the stay-at-home sort of chap, **home brewing** could be just the answer.

I have had first-hand experience with this hobby. Both my parents used to brew their own wine and beer using the airing cupboard to house the demijohns of fermenting liquid. As a child, my clothes always had the faint aroma of yeast or wine. I must have smelt like some juvenile delinquent.

My mother kept her bubbling demijohns of wine in a small cupboard under the stairs, next to the gas meter. When I got older, we had regular tastings of the cloudy mixture. It was strong enough to strip the enamel off your teeth.

Later still, I boarded for a while in France, with an aged widow from Paris. She brewed "eau de vie", an evil concoction that requires a licence to brew it. I mumbled something about my mother brewing wine and found myself in her large cellar for the next three weeks, learning the secrets of how to make proper eau de vie, quite possibly the most potent drink on the planet next to absinthe. Madame had a formidable reputation for making some of the finest eau de vie. Each Thursday, the local gendarmes visited her, not to caution her for brewing such evil stuff, but to sit down and enjoy a small glass as an aperitif before they clocked off for lunch.

She gave me a large bottle to take back to the UK for my father, who took one slug of the stuff and couldn't speak for fifteen minutes.

So, back to home brewing; you can buy easy-to-use kits so you don't need to go out and collect hops or grapes. No worries about taking off your socks and pounding the grapes with your feet in the bath, because these kits come in cans. If you are desperate to encourage your Grumpy outside for a while, send him to collect berries so he can brew his own special variety. Just about any type of berry will make a wine of sorts.

Make sure he doesn't leave it in the airing cupboard though. You don't want to smell as if you had a Chablis Smoothie for breakfast.

How about **horseball**? Horseball is performed on horseback and is like a mixture of polo, rugby, and basketball, according to Wikipedia. I wonder how the horses slam dunk those balls into the net.

Unfortunately, the weather in this country isn't the best for my favourite out of the list above: **hot-air ballooning**. A very keen Grumpy could be the next Richard Branson and balloon all around the world. Test him out by singing the Andy William's song *Up, Up and Away*, and then give him the present of a balloon flight. He'll enjoy the peace and quiet as he floats over the countryside. It won't take much to encourage him to take up this hobby. The thought of being away from the rest of the mad world below should do it. (Those burners are noisy though.)

Once smitten by this exhilarating hobby, he'll need to obtain his pilot's licence and purchase a balloon. He will then be allowed to participate in one of the many festivals for balloonists. The best known of these is the Bristol festival, held annually in August, where approximately one hundred hot air balloons attempt to lift off at the same time. It's a long shot, but you never know, this hobby might take off for him.

Are you feeling sleepy yet? That probably means you have read too much today, or that your GOM has already begun his new hobby of **hypnotism**.
You can learn how to hypnotise someone from a YouTube video. How cool is that? Unfortunately, after I watched it, I kept clucking like a chicken. You could send your fellow on a course to learn how to hypnotise people. Better still, send him to be hypnotised. You could have him transformed from a Grumpy into a Happy.

Although they no longer run across the channel, **hovercrafts** continue to fascinate people, especially GOMs. An engineer, Dirk Lohry from Dakota, recently built his own hovercraft out of a kit, for about $30,000. He can now travel over land, sea and ice at approximately 35–55mph. A hovercraft could be useful for getting about after all the rain we've had this year. Being pricey as they are, your frustrated engineer can still find fun in making a small hovercraft using duct tape, superglue, a spill proof cap from a water bottle, a plastic lid, an old CD, and a balloon. Although I rather like hovercrafts, I would prefer my Grump learned the art of hoovering and took the vacuum cleaner out once a week.

We recently found an abandoned hub cap on the side of the road when we were out walking. Mr G recognised its make immediately, which led me to check out the next hobby: **hub-cap collecting**. There are some true enthusiasts out there, and I discovered one man who has a collection of 30,000 hub caps. You'll require adequate space to store them, and don't let him collect them from moving vehicles.

On the final home stretch here with the last suggestion in this section. This is an excellent hobby and one that can be enjoyed by you both: **holidays**. I'm sure you don't require any suggestions as to where you should go. The world is your oyster these days, and even if you are on a strict budget, there is always the option of house swapping. Why are you still reading this book? You should be packing.

There are plenty of interesting ideas beginning with the letter I. Try **ice skating** or **ice sculpting**. Now, that's a hobby for someone who wishes to be individual. First, you'll need to buy a huge freezer to make lots of enormous blocks of ice for your Grumpy to practise on. Actually, no, you won't, because this is more popular than you may think.

The art of ice sculpting originated with French chefs more than 200 years ago. They used it as a method of keeping food fresh and cold by carving basins out of ice. The art was then taken up by the Russians at around the beginning of the 18th century, followed by the Japanese towards the end of the 20th century, who are now considered to be the masters of this art form. Many other countries around the world followed, including America and Canada. America has an organisation known as The National Ice Carving Association with over 500 members.

London hosts a large ice-sculpting festival, with an Ice Graffiti Wall where adults can "release the inner Banksy" on a specially constructed wall, play in a snow pit, play ice chess, and enjoy music, no doubt by Ice Cube, Vanilla Ice and Ice T.

There are courses, including master classes, available all over the country, with some notably good classes in London.

You wouldn't think that a great Victorian engineer born in 1806 would still be of continued interest for children and adults alike, yet **Isambard Kingdom Brunel**, a civil engineer and designer of major importance during the industrial revolution, holds a deep fascination for those interested in history. Is your GOM one of them?

In 2002, a public television poll conducted by the BBC to select the 100 Greatest Britons placed Brunel second, behind Winston Churchill. In the opening ceremony for the 2012 Olympic Games held in London, Kenneth Branagh portrayed Isambard Kingdom Brunel in a segment about the industrial revolution.

Okay, here are some IKB facts to wow your Grumpy:

- Brunel designed and was chief engineer on the Clifton Suspension Bridge.
- He was chief engineer at the Monkwearworth Docks at Bristol, the Great Western Railway, the Great Western steamship, the Great Britain steamship and the great Eastern steamship.
- He helped his father, Marc Brunel, to build the Thames Tunnel under the river.
- He died in 1859.
- Brunel smoked over forty cigars a day, kept in a purpose-made bag, which he carried with him at all times.

I wasn't too interested in those facts, but when I ran them past my other half, his eyes lit up, and he scurried off to find his old Meccano set hidden in the attic. You can send your man to visit some of Brunel's most famous achievements. He can spend hours on the railways alone. There are exhibitions too, or you could just settle for an Isambard Kingdom Brunel Trivia Quiz to keep him entertained.

Back now to the idea of exercise, here's one that doesn't strain the joints, provides a workout for all muscle groups, and can be performed in the front room: **indoor rowing**. It is estimated that around 500,000 people use a rowing machine each week in the UK alone.

If you can afford to purchase a rowing machine for the grumbling one, then buy a machine with a screen, so he can pretend he is in a proper rowing race. Men, being naturally competitive, will work harder and stick to something longer if they want to win. Why not make it even more realistic, and present a cup or a printed out Certificate of Achievement at the end of the rowing season to your Number One Grump?

You can get him to race more authentically. (No, not down the Thames River with the Oxford boat crew.) Gyms all over the country run Concept II rowing contests at various times of the year. The first world championship for indoor rowing took place in 1982. Huge contests occur annually in Birmingham and London, attracting hundreds of people who gather and row simultaneously in one large stadium. The world's biggest indoor rowing event in 2010 at the National Indoor Arena in Birmingham saw around 3,000 entrants competing in different weight and age categories.

Mr John Hogson was one of them. From Leeds, he only took up rowing when he was 90 and could no longer run competitively. In 2010, he was the only competitor in the over 100s category. Guess he won then.

Added bonus: with your Grumpy's newfound muscular strength from all that rowing, he'll be able to wash all those windows that need doing in your house, and he'll be able to carry all the shopping bags to the car for you.

Recently, my Grumpy has taken to mimicking personalities. He's not bad at it. In fact, he does a jolly good impression of Prince Charles and another of Paul McCartney. The only snag is that he does them often. I mean often. In fact, he does them several times a day. Now, he needs a few new ones, because my facial muscles ache with the false smile I have to give him each time he does them. That led me on to checking out the hobby, if indeed that is the right terminology, of **impersonations**, not to be confused with impressionists who were a group of painters in the 19th century in France. Yes, I admit to Googling the wrong word to start with.

The website www.ehow.com has some advice on how to perfect impressions, and claims anyone can do it with practice. They suggest you "Spend a long time listening closely to the person you'll impersonate." Good—that will keep Mr G busy as he watches all the old *Carry On* films.

They recommend you record your voice, play it back and then perfect it. That will also keep him busy. Allow extra time then, for him to buy a voice recorder, and learn how to operate it. Finally, they suggest you try it out on friends and family. Yes, what a good idea, getting Mr Grumpy to perform in front of his mother-in-law and children. Maybe skip that last step, and just indulge him by listening and cheering him on when he tries out his new skill.

Check first that your Grumpy will be suitable for this challenge by saying "Frank Spencer". If he comes back with an impression of the character from the 1970s' comedy *Some Mothers Do 'Av 'Em* and replies "Mmm Betty", this activity will suit him.

Of course, you could just settle for buying him a box set of John Culshaw or Alistair McGowan or even *Spitting Image* DVDs and let him chuckle on his own.

For men who require even more stimulation or challenge, other hobbies beginning with the letter I include **indoor rock climbing, ice fishing, Indian food, Italian art**, becoming an **Irish music enthusiast**, or better still, **Irish dancing**. Can't you picture your GOM having a jig to *Riverdance*? It would be worth it for the amusement factor alone.

I discovered some suggestions that men should take up **interior design**. I leave that choice to you, with a little word of caution. My friend's husband enjoyed his new hobby of interior design so much, he got carried away with enthusiasm, and she had to wear sunglasses to walk into the kitchen. It ended up bright canary yellow and puke green. Taking it up doesn't mean they are any good at it.

J

Last Tuesday, I was driving along a country lane and came up behind a rather fit-looking man. As I passed him, I realised he was probably in his early seventies, and yet was running like a young man. He was red in the face, but his pace was good, and he looked in excellent shape.

Jogging can have major benefits for your Grumpy, but if your Grumpy is like mine, he'll have the same response mine did as we passed the gentleman in question. "Stupid idiot. He'll kill himself with that sort of exertion!"

If jogging is a non-starter, then I am guessing you won't be able to interest him in **judo** either, although the thought of being able to take on the little hooligans who populate the local bus shelter and throw them across the road the next time they huddle together swearing loudly on their mobile phones might encourage him to try out a few sessions. "Hiee-YA!"

Judo isn't just for men, and the Olympic Games in London in 2012 saw Gemma Gibbons gaining Britain's first judo medal in 12 years.

The world's oldest female Judo master is 99-year-old Keiko Fukuda. She has been practising since the 1930s. This diminutive lady, based in San Francisco, is the first female and only one of four living judo masters to earn the highest judo honour: a tenth degree black belt. Her three fellow tenth dans are way over 80 now.

Judo is a great cardiovascular workout. It also improves strength, as a result of trying to control and dictate the movement of the opponent, and increases flexibility. You don't need to buy much equipment, just a judogi (uniform).

With benefits like that and some gentle persuasion from you, Grumpy could soon know his "ippon" from his "waza", and those hoodies in the bus shelter will shrink away when they see him walking down the road.

Taking this one step further, you could sign him up for a

course in learning **Japanese**. Language learning is excellent training for the brain, even better than those Sudoku puzzles we attempt while sitting in the garden centre, drinking coffee and reading a copy of *The Daily Mail*. Forget French. That's far too easy. Let him sink his teeth into a proper language, one that is so difficult he has to learn a whole new alphabet to even read it. Surprisingly, it is a language that I found quite easy to speak, once I got my head around all those kanji. When he becomes fluent in it or inspired by the fascinating culture behind the language, you may even be able to convince him to take you to Japan to see the astonishing spring blossoms.

Those dark nights in winter are the worst time for a grumpy old bear. He can't go outside and tend to his garden. He can't wash his car. There are too many silly shoppers in town buying up "festive rubbish". He can't even go for a walk unless he wears a luminous jacket, or he'll be knocked over by eager people leaving work and attempting to reach home at breakneck speed.

Introduce him to an absorbing housebound hobby. Buy him a **jigsaw puzzle**. I don't mean one of those 1000-piece jigsaws—that's too easy. Think big, and buy him the jigsaw puzzle that was unveiled last year as the world's largest jigsaw puzzle.

It's about eighteen feet long, so you'll have to move all the furniture out of your sitting room (and dining room) to accommodate it. With 32,256 pieces, all measuring just half an inch, the puzzle is truly fiendish. It was designed by the pop graffiti artist Keith Haring, manufactured by Ravensburger, and is called *Double Respect*. Although it has just seven colours in it, including thousands of pieces of pure white, the jigsaw company believe there are enough enthusiasts who brave this gargantuan masterpiece. Is your Grumpy one of them? I have a feeling mine would try to throw it out of the window in frustration, but since it weighs 17kg, that might prove to be a hobby in itself.

Here's an idea ... buy your Grumpy three squidgy balls and a book on how to **juggle**. I taught myself to juggle years ago, when I was a bored teenager. I used the fruit in my mother's fruit bowl. It took her four months to work out why all her apples were always bruised. She blamed the greengrocer at first, and marched downtown to tell him his fruit was of inferior quality. The poor man didn't know how to respond to my formidable mother as she waved her brown apples at him. Thereafter, she purchased her fruit from the supermarket, and when that mysteriously started to turn brown too, she used her expert detective skills to work out why. I was then banned from juggling.

Nowadays, you can buy juggling kits and go on circus skill courses to learn the art of juggling. It is addictive, and keeps friends and neighbours entertained when you perform for them. Watch out for low ceilings. You don't want little dents left all over them from the balls. Finally, do not let him practise the art using knives, your best china cups or small pets.

I was interested to discover this next hobby, as I thought it went out of fashion after the Middle Ages—**jousting**. My knowledge of history is limited, but I know that the term 'joust' is derived from Old French *joster*, which meant "to approach, to meet".

It was popular in Europe throughout the 16th century, although it was discontinued in France in 1559 after the death of King Henry II in an accident.

It has enjoyed a limited revival since the 1990s, and an American reality television show entitled *Full Metal Jousting* features contestants split into two teams of eight competing in full contact competitive jousting. The contestants are eliminated one by one until only one remains. That lucky winner wins $100,000. Tempted now to get your knight in rusty armour to train and enter?

The upside of being a Grumpy is that you are, at times, extremely funny. There are moments when GOMs come out with statements that make you fall about laughing. If there is the tiniest spark of humour in your man, you must encourage him to take up telling **jokes**. Stand-up is not out of the question. After all, 90-year-old Chelsea pensioner, Jack Woodward, lived a lifelong dream in a Channel 4 documentary when he revived his career and became Britain's oldest stand-up comedian.

Laughter has long been known to be the best medicine. I won't 'bang on' about all the benefits of laughter, but there are many, and that is why I write humorous novels. I recently read, but don't ask me where because I can't remember at all, that an average healthy child laughs approximately four hundred times a day and a grown adult laughs approximately fifteen times a day. I'm not sure how often a Grumpy laughs in a day, but it is probably fair to say fifteen times a week is pushing it.

However, I stand by the statement, "He who laughs … lasts". It's a fact that laughter can release endorphins, which create a feel-good factor. Laughter gives your abdominal muscles a great workout, and most importantly, laughter will stop your Grumpy from becoming too depressed.

Try and get him to read daily jokes on websites, or tell him a few over breakfast. Laugh at all of his jokes, and he will start telling more. Eventually, with the right direction and handling, you'll have a comedian on your hands.

I found this wonderful piece of advice on the internet. "Jokes, comedy shows, and family games where improvising is involved are just a number of ways for having fun. Set up a date where you and your family can get together, and have a night of fun and laughter. Put on some comedy shows in the living room, get busy with some jokes in the kitchen and find a place to play some role playing comedy with your family and friends.

One fun game is where everyone takes turns to imitate a profession, action, or person. Without talking or giving hints through speech, the person who is standing must try to act as what he has chosen to be. For example, if one were to try to imitate an electrician he would try and pretend he is playing with wires or fake getting an electric jolt. Then everyone else tries to be the first to guess what that person is imitating, the one who does guess it first then becomes the one who must stand up and role-play.

Whatever you can do to laugh more and have some fun is good; give yourself some time, and do as much as possible. It's just one of those things that will keep you healthy."[3]

You may be sceptical about a true Grumpy joining in with that little game; but there is a reason I mentioned it—I once took my Grumpy on a laughter course. Yes, a course to make you laugh. You can imagine the comments he made before I got him there, kicking and screaming.

After lying on the floor faking laughter until it became real, then playing some very silly games that made us all chuckle so much we coughed, my Grumpy declared he felt much better (for a while) and even managed to smile for a whole afternoon. Try it out, after all, what have you got to lose?

Other hobbies or interests beginning with jolly letter J include **jukeboxes** (a Wurlitzer in the lounge—how grand!), **jazz**, **jet skiing**, **jam making**, and **Joe 90**. I'll leave you to ponder what they might get up to if they are interested in that last one.

3   *Disabled World—Disability News for all the Family,*
http://www.disabled-world.com/artman/publish/elderly-hobbies.shtml#ixzz2BrBDk0Ql

K

The letter K does not offer an abundance of choices for keeping your grouch out of mischief. But one obvious interest is **karaoke**. Who doesn't love a good sing-along? There are karaoke games for X Box or Playstation, or even CDs with no actual singing, so you can be the artist and howl along to the backing track. (Just like me.) Better still, get him along to the local pubs to participate in their Karaoke evening. Should he display any talent in this direction, encourage this hobby. There might be prize money involved, and he could even go on to form a band with other talented Grumpies like the Grumpy Old Men Rock and Blues Band, whom I recently discovered on Facebook.

If, like my own Grump, yours is tone deaf but loves chocolate, try him out with **Kinder Eggs**. He might become addicted to more than just the chocolate. I have discovered a whole bunch of men who not only collect the toys found in the eggs, but trade them and write about them in blogs.

I came across one gentleman, Thore from Sweden, who has an incredible collection of 7,000 Kinder Surprise toys. He first started collecting when his young daughters came across some cute hand-painted Kinder figures at a market in the 1990s. He helped the girls find more of the toys and soon they realised they had a large collection. Years later, he has a huge collection, which he displays in cabinets. His website, updated and kept by his daughter, is well worth a visit: www.thore.se

K is also for **karate**, **keep fit**, and **Kung Fu**. Your man must have seen 1984 film *The Karate Kid*, in which a handyman/ martial-arts master agrees to teach karate to a bullied boy. You haven't? Rent it, and then encourage your man to take up this hobby.

In the film, the karate master, Mr Miyagi, played by Noriyuki 'Pat' Morita has his student, Daniel LaRusso, played by Ralph Macchio, perform laborious chores such as sanding a wooden floor, refinishing a fence, waxing cars, and painting his house.

Unbeknown to Daniel, each chore is accompanied with a specific movement, such as clockwise/counter clockwise hand motions. Eventually, Miyagi reveals Daniel has been learning defensive blocks through muscle memory learned by performing the chores. You can see where I am going with this now, can't you? If you are cunning, you'll be able to get your man to undertake any number of household tasks and yet convince him he is learning to improve his muscles for karate. Just yell, "wax on, wax off" at him if he slows down. He'll understand.

If that doesn't convince him, then the idea that he could chop logs using the back of his hand, thus saving a fortune on a saw, must have appeal. Here are some tempting facts to enthuse him:

- Clint Poore set a new record in 2012 when he karate chopped fourteen Pop Tarts.
- Ed Byrne from Cornwall chopped through fifty-five granite and concrete edging stones in 4.86 seconds using only the palm of his hand.
- In Turkey, Ali Bahcetepe chopped 1,135 concrete blocks in one minute.

Keep fit is a must. I have touched on it under the heading Exercise.

Kung Fu is yet another martial art. I get mixed up with them all. I remember watching David Carradine in the television series *Kung Fu* in the 1970s. It seemed to involve a lot of patience, so I ruled it out as a possible for my own Mr G. "Ah, Grasshopper!"

Get a copy of *Kung Fu Panda*, and I am sure that will help clarify the situation. If it doesn't, at least you'll have been amused for a while. Kung Fu academies are to be found all over the UK and the world.

K is for **knitting**. Is this appropriate for your man? I think it could be. My research unveiled a surprising number of groups and forums for men who knit. Some of them have blogs about knitting, and all are extremely enthusiastic about the craft. Point your man to www.menwhoknit.com or www.madmanknitting. wordpress.com to show him that this is not just a pastime for women. You can also throw in the name of Barry Klein, who is the owner of Trendsetter Yarns and past president of the National Needlework Association. He has designed patterns for Vogue Knitting, Interweave Knits, and Knitters magazine.

Encourage your Grumpy to take up this hobby, and you'll never have to buy him socks for Christmas again.

For that little grouch who needs extra love in his life, get him a pet. Buy him some **Koi Carp**. He'll need a pond too. Koi are ornamental varieties of domesticated common carp that are kept for decorative purposes in outdoor koi ponds. Koi Carp Magazine has a wealth of information about these pretty fish, and offers a variety of gifts, including a T-shirt that says "Keep Calm and Keep Koi". As we know, all Grumpies need to keep calm. This could be the answer.

Korfball is a game that originated in Holland. Korfball World Championships and European Championships are held every four years. There are numerous clubs and leagues in Great Britain, so you should be able to sign him up for some lessons. It is, in essence, a team sport. Teams are made up of four men and four women. In fact, it is the only team game in the world in which they have mixed gender players.

The game is usually played indoors on a 40m x 20m court. The idea is to shoot the ball through the opponent's basket, which is made out of rattan and called a "korf" (Dutch for "basket"). Games last one hour and are split into two thirty-minute halves. So, here you have it, a hobby you can enjoy together, unless you are both extremely competitive.

Finally, if you need a more adventurous activity for your other half, then check out **kiteboarding**. Also known as **kitesurfing**, it has been described as combining wakeboarding, windsurfing, surfing, paragliding, and gymnastics into one extreme sport.

Poul Rasmusson, the world's oldest kitesurfer, died in October 2012 while riding his eight metre kite near Copenhagen, a few kilometres from his house, at the age of 88. It would appear that age is not a barrier to this sport. Besides, wouldn't your Grumpy look good in a wet suit? In July 2012, Richard Branson became the oldest man to kitesurf the English Channel. If it's good enough for Richard ...

L is for **looking around for something to do**, or to hang out with somebody. Let's hope some of these suggestions prove helpful and get Mr G out of the way for a while.

"La plume de ma tante et dans le train." Ah! Those happy days of learning French at school where Mme Boulevard would only speak in her native tongue, and say, "Oh là là!" at every opportunity. Now is an ideal time for your Grumpy to learn not just French but any language he fancies; Mandarin, Japanese or Swahili. It has never been easier to **learn a language** either. There are an abundance of courses, available at bookshops, evening classes, and day classes or just from the internet. The BBC site alone offers a glut of languages from Arabic to Urdu.

Being a linguist, this is a subject I am passionate about. Language learning is better for your brain than puzzles, and dare I say it, more useful. Just imagine it, you are on holiday in Mexico, Hubby will be able to translate the menu and order all the food for you, without you having to point at the menu and shout at the waiter in English.

Steve Kaufmann, who founded The Linguist Institute, started learning Russian—his ninth language—when he was 60 years old and then learned Portuguese at 62.

Never mind languages, how about just **learning**? Your Grumpy has all the time in the world to complete a course, or even a degree. Don't let him tell you his mind is too old. Many people think that as you age you forget things and daydream more. Scientists have proved that learning helps keep the synapses in the brain functioning and can keep your brain from ageing. (Sorry—what was I talking about?)

When I was a student at university, one of my class members was a retired lady. She passed with first-class honours (which is more than I did—should have spent less time in the student's bar). Take also the example of 98-year-old Nola Ochs, who graduated at Fort Hays University with a master's degree, having only obtained her bachelor degree three years earlier at the age of 95.

Check out evening classes at your local college. He might be pleasantly surprised at what is on offer and even find a few like-minded retired fellow Grumps there to help him with his homework.

We touched upon doing the rumba, cha cha and **Latin dancing** earlier, so I'll leap through a few other possibilities now: **leather crafts**, **lead toy soldiers**, **literature**, **local history**, **listening to music**, **lathe work**, or—and this is a 'different' one—**log rolling**, which involves two lumberjacks, each on one end of a log floating in the river. One or the other starts "walking" (or "rolling") the log and the other is forced to keep up. The contest involves staying on the log while attempting to cause the competitor to lose their balance and splash into the water. You will probably have to send Grumpy abroad for that particular activity and make sure he has plenty of towels to dry himself with.

A slightly more viable option is **land yachting** (also called sand yachting, land sailing, and sand surfing). This is a sporting activity, which will appeal to your grouchy man because it only uses wind power; ergo, it is a cheap activity. A land yacht is essentially a three- wheeled vehicle with a large yacht's sail and is often home-built. Already, I can foresee fun and frolics in the garage as he attempts to read the instructions, glasses perched on end of nose, assembling his new toy. He could cheat and buy a commercially built one, but where's the fun in that?

Land yachts can reach significantly high speeds, the current world record being 116 mph. He will require a land-yachting pilot's licence if he wishes to go racing with it. Best used on a long beach. I'll leave you to imagine what would happen if he took it out to the local supermarket car park.

Here's an innovative idea to brighten up the summer months for your dear old Grump: **lawn mower racing**. This rather bizarre activity originated in West Sussex in 1973 in a pub. (What a surprise!)

As with all vaguely ridiculous ideas, it took off, and now there are races throughout the UK and Europe. It is very high-profile in the USA—it's even televised regularly—and is run by the US Lawn Mower Racing Association. Don't knock it, because past winning teams have included well-known professional racing drivers Sir Stirling Moss and Derek Bell. There is also a World Championship and a British Championship, which includes a twelve-hour team endurance race. I wonder if I could get them to host it in my garden next year. It could do with a good cut. Lend your GOM out to neighbours so he can try out his machine and earn beer money at the same time.

LEGO continues to hold fascination for men and women of all ages. The famous LEGO brick is over fifty years old, so there is every chance your Grumpy will have played with this toy at some stage in his life. Test him with these fascinating facts, and see if you can get him to relive those happy childhood days by building some LEGO toys.

- LEGO is an abbreviation of the two Danish words leg godt (play well).
- A column of about 40,000,000,000 LEGO bricks would reach the moon.
- On average every person on earth has sixty-two LEGO bricks.
- There are 915 million ways to combine six LEGO bricks.
- Approximately seven LEGO sets are sold each second.
- The LEGO Club has 2.4 million members worldwide.[4]

"Yee haw!" How about dressing up your Grumpy in a pair of cowboy boots and trying out **line-dancing**? There are classes all over the UK. George Lombardi is still line-dancing at 100 years old. He can be found on the dance floor of the Colorado Cafe in Watchung, line-dancing alongside hundreds of others. He attends classes twice a week, proof you are never too old to strut your stuff.

question: how many line dance instructors does it take to change a light bulb?
answer: five! six! seven! eight!

4   http://www.webuser.co.uk/websites/online-fun-blog/websites/393104/10-amazing-lego-facts

There are some magical ideas for interests beginning with the letter M. These include **music, model making, magic, marbles, maps, motorbikes, motor scooters, mountain bikes, mountaineering** (you are never too old— Mount Everest was climbed by Yuichiro Miura at the age of 70), **mushrooms** (growing and collecting them, rather than scoffing them—make sure he learns the difference between mushrooms and poisonous toadstools early on in this hobby, and double check that he doesn't inadvertently pick up some "magic" hallucinogenic mushrooms and end up having a grumpy old trip), **music boxes, mud fishing**, and **murder mystery weekends**.

Tempted as I am to encourage you to get your Grumpy to take up **Morris dancing**, I am going to suggest **Molly dancing** instead. This is a type of East Anglian ritual dance, similar to Morris dancing, but without the sticks. One may feel that a Grumpy wheedling a stick and threatening to whack his partner with it could lead to dire consequences. In Molly dancing, the participants wave hankies and bells instead of sticks, and shout a lot—much more suitable for a miserable old grump, even though they wear face paint and bright clothes.

The dance steps in Molly dancing are also different to those of Morris dancing. Molly dancing is associated with the annual Plough Monday tradition occurring on the first Monday after twelfth night, during which young farm hands would drag a plough around local villages while shouting "penny for the ploughboys". If they didn't receive a penny, they dug a furrow across the property owner's front lawn. (Don't let your Grump take this hobby to heart and attempt this.) This part of the festivities took place after dark, but during the daytime, the local Molly dancers would tour the region dancing and collecting money.

did you hear the joke about the
magician who got so mad he pulled
his hare out?

what about the magician who loved
chocolate? he performed a lot of
twix.

All of this nonsense leads me nicely onto this possibility: **magic**. No one is too old to learn magic. Small magic tricks can be purchased from shops or online. There are a number of groups and advice on the internet to help your Grumpy become a proficient magician.

The oldest magic trick is believed to have been a conjuring trick using a cup and balls, possibly performed in Egypt around 2700 BCE. (Before the Common/Current/Christian Era.) The Magic Circle, which ensures magicians don't give away the secrets of their magic, was formed in 1905, and in 1994, magic stores and websites appeared on the World Wide Web, changing the way magic is learned and distributed.

We moved house last year, and needed some new curtains and blinds. A team of father and son came to fit them. The father, an elderly gentleman, had come to help hold poles and the like. It transpired he had taken up magic when he retired, and now gave performances for children's birthday parties and small gatherings. He spent all morning showing us his tricks. We stood open-mouthed. The curtains, meanwhile, all went up without him lifting his finger to help. "Now that's magic!"

You can lose more than just balls in cups (did you like the way I attempted to link into this paragraph just then?) and purchasing your Grumpy a **metal detector** could lead to some surprising discoveries. In 2009, a housewife found a hoard of fifteenth-century gold, worth £250,000 using a metal detector. In June 2012, a pair of metal-detector friends found three quarters of a ton of Iron Age coins, worth £10m, buried in a field in Jersey. The coins had been buried to protect them from Julius Caesar.

The two friends had searched the field for three decades before they discovered them—but what a find!

Metal detecting forums, websites, magazines and equipment are readily available. Detectors start around £24.99 and obviously increase in price depending on their capabilities. Imagine your pleasure if you could lose your Grumpy regularly for three decades in a field, and then become a few million pounds richer.

He needs to be careful where he goes with his new toy, though. Some people can be rather funny about where you are carrying out your detecting. Take the example of Graham Grubster, who was out detecting in a field one day, when a couple of walkers started giving him grief.

"You shouldn't be here," they yelled. "We know the farmer, and he didn't give you permission." They set off to find the farmer and alert him to the presence of the man on his land. They couldn't find him, so they called the police. Two officers duly arrived, took Graham's details and went off to check him out. They came back full of apologies. "Sorry, Graham," they said, "we didn't realise you were the landowner."

Monopoly is one of the most popular board games of all time. I have already mentioned board games, but I felt this was worthy of bringing up here, since many Grumpy Old Men like to be in control of money. Therefore, this game has added appeal for them. Don't worry, you don't have to sit with him while he triumphantly builds hotels on Mayfair and demands you bankrupt yourself. He can do it all online, where there are several sites he can join and play others.

There is more to it than just playing the board game. How about a Monopoly pub crawl? Yes, your Grumpy can do a pub crawl, attempting to drink a half pint in every one of 26 pubs (game players prefer to finish the route rather than pass out halfway round) that follow the designated Monopoly Pub Crawl route. It is a fun day out for your Grumpy. Check out their website for further details.

Finally, you can send him to McDonalds when they do their annual Monopoly promotion, which lasts a month. He can not only play Monopoly, but he might even win a Big Mac for dinner.

McDonalds is listed as an interest or hobby. More accurately, collecting McDonald toys issued as promotions in Happy Meals is a hobby or interest. Started in 1979 to increase sales, the first toy to appear in a Happy Meal was a Circus Wagon Train. The popularity of these meals and toys grew, not just among children, but adults, too.

Some collectors concentrate on specialist areas for their collection. These might include pins, badges or telephone cards. Others collect themes such as Star Wars or Disney. The most popular items offered in the Happy Meals were Barbie Dolls and Matchbox cars.

The UK McDonalds Collectors Club was started in 2001. There is also an annual convention for the thousand plus members each year. (I wonder if they turn up dressed as clowns.)

I hope he takes up this hobby, after all; there is something appealing about the idea of a Grumpy sitting down with a Happy Meal.

I shall skip over the other interests above to mention one that has enormous appeal for grumbling, yet creative, men. This is probably due to the fact they played with it as children: **Meccano**. Small sets are readily available in shops and online, as are periodicals, manuals and clubs that your man can join.

Meccano was invented by Frank Hornby in 1901, and was originally called 'Mechanics Made Easy'. It has enjoyed undying popularity over the years. Your Grumpy will undoubtedly regard it with fondness—or complain that today's sets aren't the same as those from yesteryear.

Some interesting facts about Meccano:

- A Chinese company plans to build the world's tallest skyscraper in just seven months using pre-fabricated components slotted together like a Meccano toy.
- One of the lesser facts about Meccano is its ability to solve mathematical problems. One example is the use of the bolted strips of metal as an analogue computer or differential analyser.
- The printed version of the *Encyclopedia of Meccano Parts* (EMP) consists of six volumes. When stacked one on top of the other, they make a pile four inches high.

Okay, I glazed over reading all those facts too. However, your man will be riveted—and just think how occupied he would be if you bought him the entire set of Encyclopaedias to read.

Of all the activities there are beginning with the letter M, the most unusual is **mudlarking**. Mudlarking, in spite of its name, doesn't seem to offer much in the way of larks or fun. Mudlarks used to search the muddy shores of the River Thames during low tide, scavenging for anything that could be resold.

Mudlarks were either youngsters aged between eight and fifteen or the robust elderly. It has made a sort of resurgence since 1980, when a modern organisation was founded. It was granted a special licence allowing its members to search the Thames mud for treasure and historical artefacts.

All finds have to be reported to The Museum of London. There are special mudlarking tours along the Thames river, should you wish to try your luck. If a trip to London is out of the question, then I guess you could send him to the local canal or river where I am sure that, like us, you'll be able to pick up a tyre and a shopping trolley at the very least.

N

Introduce your man to **needlepoint**. Before you stare at this in amazement and think "Surely not?" let me tell you about Roosevelt "Rosey" Grier, an American actor, singer, Christian minister and former professional American football player. After a successful sports career, he worked as a bodyguard for Robert Kennedy during the 1968 presidential campaign, and was guarding the senator's wife, Ethel Kennedy, during the Robert F Kennedy assassination. It was Roosevelt Grier who took control of the gun and subdued the shooter.

This isn't a history lesson as such, I just wanted to explain that any man can be interested in needlepoint, and Grier is known for his serious pursuit of hobbies not normally associated with men, such as macramé and needlepoint. He has even written several books about them, including Needlepoint for Men (1973). Born in July 1932, this remarkable man is now 80 years old. Now try letting your Grumpy bat this hobby away, declaring it to be for women.

Following the theme of sports or activities normally associated with women, how about **netball**? I found out last week that every female netball team is allowed to have one male member. Further delving brought up interesting facts about men who now play netball. It originated in Australia, the land of testosterone-fuelled men who cook "barbies" and drink "tinnies". Somehow, that seems to make it acceptable. I wonder if they have to wear those awful gym skirts like we did when we were at school. If you can convince your Grumpy to take it up, then you are a better woman than me. Mine refused point-blank to even consider it.

Interest your Grumpy in **1950s' memorabilia**, **1960s' memorabilia**, or **1970s' memorabilia** (are you detecting a pattern yet?). There are oodles of memorabilia to be purchased on eBay or in stores, especially antique stores, flea markets, garage sales, car boot sales ... the list is endless.

It is best if he focuses on certain items, like records from a particular decade, or sweets or toys, otherwise you'll need a larger home to house all his collection. It can become completely addictive, and not only could he collect memorabilia from a certain decade, but you could host parties themed around that decade.

Retrieve the flared trousers and velvet jackets from the attic, and host a themed seventies night, where you can relive those days of Space Hoppers, lava lamps, and great music. Sing along to *Bye Bye Baby* from The Bay City Rollers or *Puppy Love* from Donny Osmond. Better still, reintroduce prawn cocktails, and cheese and pineapple on sticks to people's palates, and don't forget the Blue Nun wine. Bet you enjoy it.

There is not a lot to choose out of activities beginning with the letter N but the last few should make your eyes light up (or water): **nude inline skating, nude rambling, nude sailing, nude skiing, or nude touch rugby**. I don't need to elaborate here. I think you get the picture. Erasing it from your mind will probably be more difficult.

○

Octopus hunting, **Orangutan spotting**, and **opium smoking** may not seem sensible choices for your Grumpy, but they are outrageous hobbies.

Should your dear old Grumpy be a clone of my own, he complains endlessly at the potholes and condition of our roads. From potholes to speed cameras and white van drivers who tailgate him, he'll chunter on every trip you take.

Treat him to an off-road experience day to let him rekindle his love for driving. **Off-road motoring** brings back the pleasure of driving and tests those skills he claims he is no longer able to use. Courses are available throughout the UK, and an old second-hand four-by-four vehicle can be picked up at a decent price.

You'll then be able to send him out for a day in the countryside attempting to navigate fords and hills, while you trundle off to town in the Yaris in peace.

In 2011, 71-year-old Arthur Boyt of Davistow won the British Night Orienteering Championships held at Bentley Woods, near Birmingham.

Unlike Arthur, I have no sense of direction. I constantly check my right from my left when giving directions, but **orienteering** could be just up your GOM's street (or even his field). Participants receive a map which they use to find control points. They require navigational skills, using the map and a compass to navigate from point to point in diverse and unfamiliar terrain, usually at speed and against the clock. I think I'll sit that one out. 'Navigation', 'dark' and 'running' in the same sentence makes me want to reach out for another chocolate biscuit.

Away from activities that create adrenalin rushes such as orienteering or **outdoor pursuit**s, and onto ones that calm. **Organ lessons** could transform your man once you stop him laughing at the suggestion or making the obvious jokes.

If not bothered about organ or **oboe playing** or even becoming part of an **orchestra**, he could try **octopush**. This worldwide underwater activity was invented in 1954 by Alan Blake of Southsea, UK, for fellow members of his aqua club, when they couldn't dive outside during winter months.

It is a form of underwater hockey, where eight members of each team push a lead weight, called a squid, across a swimming pool floor with sticks into goals. It has gained popularity throughout Britain and the world. Originally, the game did not involve the use of snorkels; it's up to you to decide whether to let your Grumpy use one.

Michael Portillo loves it, my mother adores it, and with the boom of *Mad Men*, retro is in, so why not seize the opportunity to be ahead of the curve, make your man cool and introduce him to **opera**. It's been the preferred entertainment choice of royalty and elite classes since the 16th century. Let's face it; anything with that longevity must have real substance. Besides, your GOM will be able to wear his old tuxedo that's been mothballing for decades and go for a proper night out, once he has studied the basics of opera and decided what he likes.

If you don't know which opera to take him to first, then here are the top three most popular operas to give you some ideas:

- *La Bohème* by Giacomo Puccini is the most performed and well liked opera of this and probably any time. It is the inspiration for the musical "Rent!" and is similar in many ways, except the people in it don't have AIDS. Instead, the lead female, Mimi, contracts TB and of course dies. Hankies required, even if you are a man.
- *Carmen* by Georges Bizet is the story of Carmen the gypsy girl and her love for Don José. Their love doesn't last long, and they start fighting (sounds like a lot of relationships today). In the end Carmen is killed. It is particularly well known for the Toreador song.

- *The Marriage of Figaro* by Wolfgang Amadeus Mozart is part two of the three series of Figaro. This opera takes place entirely in one day in Count Almaviva's Palace. It is a tale of mistaken identities, and excellent comedy is woven throughout the opera. Even an old misery should appreciate it.

OPERA IS WHEN A GUY GETS STABBED IN THE BACK, AND INSTEAD OF BLEEDING, HE SINGS.

Alternatively, try interesting him in **orchids**, collecting **old hand tools** (he probably already has a collection of those), developing an interest in **Oriental items** such as carpets, swords, daggers, or ceramics; or sit him down with a large pile of paper and let him become absorbed in the art of origami, also known as paper folding.

The **Origami** Paper Club website claims to be the "most popular website on the planet", so he'll have plenty of fellow hobbyists.

The most common known item to make in origami is a crane—the bird variety, not the mechanical one often to be seen on building sites. A 207-foot-tall crane was made in Japan in 1998, but the world's largest paper crane was created in 1999 in Seattle, USA, by Wings for Peace. It was over 215-feet wide and weighed approximately 1750 pounds.

I USED TO WORK IN AN ORIGAMI STORE BUT IT FOLDED. (I BET THAT JOKE HAD YOU IN CREASES.)

There are quite a few online activities that Grumpy Guts could take up. I have already mentioned blogging earlier, but there is also **online chatting, online gaming, online music, online social networking** and finally, **online dating**. I wouldn't be too quick to offer up that particular choice though.

Oil painting, like other art forms, is productive and calming. The first ever oil paintings were found in Afghanistan. They date back to 650 AD.

Oil paints dry to the touch within two weeks, and are generally dry enough to be varnished in six months to a year. This allows the artist time to work on them after initially painting them. It may take years for a painting to dry completely. I only mention that in case you should accidentally sit on one of your man's masterpieces while wearing white trousers.

My last offering for activities or interests beginning with the letter O comes from a very popular British comedy series broadcast in the 1980s, **Only Fools and Horses**. This is not just an excuse to sit down with a large box set of the DVDs. There is a vast range of memorabilia and collector's items available.

A convention is held each year in England, where some members of the original cast attend giving out free autographs, and lookalike actors recreate classic scenes. There is also an *Only Fools and Horses* Appreciation Society.

Keep your fingers crossed that he doesn't go in search of a three-wheeled yellow Robin Reliant van.

P

The letter P produces a preposterous list of possibilities, from **pram racing** to **parahawking**.

Do you remember the old chimpanzee adverts for a well-known brand of tea on television? Here are a few fascinating facts about **PG Tips**:

- An average cup of PG tips is virtually fat free.
- It is second only to water as being the best drink to hydrate with.
- An average cup of PG tips contains only half the caffeine of an average cup of freshly brewed coffee.
- Tea, like PG tips, contains fluoride, which may be beneficial to your dental health.

I am not, however, proposing you introduce your significant other to tea drinking as a hobby. I'm suggesting he collects the picture cards you used to find in boxes of this beverage.

PG Tips tea picture cards have been appearing in packets of PG Tips since 1954. The first issue of cards in 1954 was a set of 50, depicting British Birds. A total of 57 sets (not all containing 50 cards) were issued in total, and in 1999, the set only had 3 cards, in "Brook Bond's Farewell to PG Tips." The final "Thank You" card—a survey card—was issued at the end of 1999.

Depending on the state and condition of your cards, some fetch good prices, and catalogues giving you approximate values can be downloaded. There is even a Facebook page for collectors of cards. Of course, if picture cards from tea boxes hold no appeal then maybe Pokémon cards will; that is, if he knows what Pokémon is.

Should your man have a desire to run around with a gun and pretend he is part of Alpha Force, then **paintballing** is ideal for him. Shopping centres often have paintballing stands manned by chaps with blacked-out faces. Book him on a day with a couple of friends. He'll be converted in no time and will be talking about 'squeegees', 'demon cockers', 'bunkered' and being 'gogged'. It's worth it just for that alone. As for age; don't worry, there are plenty of men in their seventies who still play.

Pole dancing. Ha! I was just testing to see if you are awake. I only put that there for fun, but now I've mentioned it, I bet you have a little smirk at the thought of your Grumpy attempting to pole dance. There are a few male pole dancers, and in 2011, Steve Retchless—or should that be "reckless"—pole danced on the America's Got Talent quarterfinals.

One of the most popular pastimes for retired people is **painting**. Here, I refer to the art version and not the painting of your living room, although that too can be absorbing. Painting is therapeutic and rewarding. Your GOM can spend time at lessons, on courses, at home and outside enjoying this activity. Please remember to put up all his artwork on the fridge so he can see how good it is.

question: why was the art dealer in debt? answer: he didn't have any monet?

Buy your Grumpy some paper and let him make **paper planes**. Not the ones he used to make at school, which he flew around the classroom and landed in front of the Maths teacher's feet when he was trying to explain equations, but more sophisticated varieties. Books and websites will instruct him as to how he may fashion all sorts of planes, including fighter paper planes.

For the adventurous sort, there are some pretty exciting activities that involve an element of danger, for example: **parachuting, paragliding, parakarting, paramotoring**, and **parasailing**.

Leonado Da Vinci sketched the first design for a parachute in 1485, although the modern parachute was invented in the late 18th century by a Frenchman, Louis-Sebastien Lenormand, who also made the first recorded public jump in 1783.

There have been various records for parachute jumping, the most recent by Felix Baumgarten, who jumped from an altitude of 128,100 feet and reached speeds of up to 833.9 mph.

Parachuting is not just for the young; a 92-year-old with artificial knees made it into the record books by becoming the oldest person to ever jump out of an airplane with a parachute.[5]

question: what do you call it when your parachute doesn't open? answer: jumping to a conclusion.

Like painting, **photography** is extremely popular among retired people. Today, with modern technology and all the software available, it is difficult to take a bad photograph. However, your Grumpy will probably moan about digital photography and how all the skill has been removed from photography, thanks to these new-fangled pieces of equipment. Should he be one of those men, buy him a Box Brownie camera and convert under the stairs into a dark room for him. He'll be deliriously happy.

Fancy listening to your Grumpy attempt to play a concerto? Get him to take up **piano** lessons. Chances are he'll get fed up trying to learn the scales and might only be able to play *Chopsticks* after ten weeks, but at least you'll have tried.

5   http://factspage.blogspot.co.uk/2010/02/10-interesting-parachute-facts.html

Rather than have a baby grand in your living room, you could opt for a **pool table**. He'll be able to learn the art of playing pool and even invite neighbours around for a game. Go the whole hog, and buy a **pinball** machine, thus transforming your dining room into a proper games room. You'll never get him out of it, and you won't have to worry about cooking meals any more.

Here are a few suggestions that I don't need to elaborate upon: **playing cards, plane spotting, poetry, pop music, pressed flowers, puppets, public speaking** and **puzzles**.

And to close the list on activities beginning with the letter P, I would like to propose **power-boat racing** and last, but not least, that marvellous activity: **prune stone spitting**. Prunes are supposed to be good for you, since they are full of antioxidants and fibre, so make sure he eats plenty of them and then uses the stones wisely to practise this activity.

Prune stone spitting competitions take place in Sainte-Livrade-sur-Lot in France each year. It is an area renowned for its prunes, and approximately one hundred competitors line up in the town centre to spit the pits. The furthest shot wins the honour of being that year's best spitter. The record stands at over twenty metres. I feel sorry for the poor wife who has to live with that competitor.

Q

QUESTION: WHAT Q CAN BAFFLE, FRUSTRATE, AND YET STILL ENTERTAIN? ANSWER: A QUIZ, OF COURSE.

Quizzes are the perfect way to spend an afternoon or evening, especially if you like trumping your partner by answering more questions than them.

There are all sorts of quizzes: pub quizzes, television quizzes, internet quizzes, or magazine quizzes. Books and magazines containing quizzes have been popular for many years, but the late eighties saw the introduction of quiz competitions in pubs.

QUESTION: WHO DOESN'T ENJOY A GOOD OLD PUB QUIZ? ANSWER: PROBABLY A GRUMPY.

He might be better suited to a more challenging quiz like *Mastermind* or *Eggheads*. Check out how to enter these shows, and get him signed up. There are so many television quizzes to have a go at that he should be very well occupied researching before each event.

There is always *Trivial Pursuit,* a game that has become so popular, there are now various editions to amuse all tastes and ages. I hope they bring out a 'Grumpy' edition. I love trivia, as you can guess from this book, so here are a few little gems to blurt out at your next Trivial Pursuit tournament:

- The house fly hums in the middle octave key of F.
- Tigers have striped skin, not just striped fur.
- Hummingbirds are the only animal that can fly backwards.
- The "dot" over the letter i is called a tittle.

The website www.manquilters.ning.com is dedicated to men who like to make quilts. It is full of fascinating stuff for men and should make your Grumpy feel part of a caring, sharing community of men who have a genuine passion for this hobby. There are pieces of advice about **quilting** festivals and how to do strip quilting(!).

Quad biking is a manly sort of activity, requiring an irritating machine that roars about up and down your drive or around your garden when you are trying to listen to the afternoon play on Radio 4.

Personally, I dislike them because they seem to be dangerous. Researching this subject produced a lot of news reports about serious injuries and deaths. I only want my Grump to be occupied and out of the house, and not, like Ozzy Osbourne, break his bones and end up seriously injured in hospital; he would make a dreadful patient.

If your man is up for some outlandish suggestions, then try him out with **quad roller skating**, quad speed skating, or just insist he calms down and plays some nice old fashioned **quoits**. This is a traditional game which involves the throwing of metal, rope or rubber rings over or near a spike. Jolly useful for when you go to a funfair and want to have a go at the hoopla stall.

I'm scraping the barrel here with the letter Q, but you could suggest classes in **quadrille**, which is a type of square dancing. Sorry, but I can't seem to find out where, other than London, you can learn this, and even then, the club in question insists you are fit and lively.

Failing that, how about trying out **Quidditch**? I hear it's all the rage in the magical world, although I'm not sure if your "muggle" Grumpy will be allowed to compete.

R

Rah, rah—I am feeling rumbustious about the letter R as it affords the average Grump a riotous choice of activity or hobby.

We can look at **rowing, running, rounders, racquetball, racing, rambling, real tennis, rock climbing, roller skating,** or **rugby.** There are so many sporting activities here, we are spoilt for choice. However, these are popular hobbies; let's think 'alternative': recreational tree **climbing** or **rabbit show jumping?** You did read that last bit correctly. The sport of training rabbits to jump over obstacles started in Sweden in 1979 and the first National Championships were held in 1986, where sixty rabbits competed.

This sport has since spread from the Scandinavian countries into Europe and as far as Japan and the States. There is also a British Championship, which is held in August each year. The rabbits compete at dressage, high jump and long jump. It might appeal to your Grump, although personally, I think the owners must be mad as March hares.

A more sensible idea involves a control panel and a stick. I am referring to **remote-controlled** vehicles. I have yet to see a grown man not enjoy operating a remote-controlled car, helicopter, or boat. It brings out the inner child in any GOM.

A *mini* Mini was used at the 2012 Olympic Games to deliver javelins, hammers, shots and discuses, loaded into the car through its sunroof, to the athletes as they got ready to compete. I bet the person who got to control it had a ball.

Your Grumpy probably has already commandeered the remote control for the television and flicks endlessly through the television channels, alighting on programmes for only a few minutes before chasing off to find a programme he prefers. Well, here is a chance to retrieve it and let him fiddle with a different variety.

"Breaker, Breaker, this is Rubber Duck!" I remember the good old days of CB radios. Your man might even be old enough to recall the Tony Hancock sketch *The Radio Ham*. What I'm suggesting here, is getting him a **radio** set. A proper one, where he can moan to fellow curmudgeons from all over the world, and discuss how bad the weather is in each country and what time it is. It's inexpensive, and information on how to go about it is readily available.

Or, you could buy him an anorak and send him to the local railway station, where he can become a **railway enthusiast**. That's an unfair comment, as railway enthusiasts often have a genuine enthusiasm for trains, electric or steam. Some even spend weekends operating old steam trains for tourists and making sure our old heritage stays alive.

Men seem to love engines. If he can play with signals or get to drive a train, you will find yourself with a very content Grumpy. You could always buy him a train set if he can't get to an interesting station. That is, if you are willing to let him set it up in the spare room or attic and wear a conductor's hat.

Encourage your Grumpy to take up **reiki** or **reflexology**, and you could be getting free relaxing treatments for life. I would only let Mr G near my feet if I were sure he wouldn't turn into a schoolboy and tickle them.

If he is a car enthusiast then he could become interested in **Renault**, **Rolls Royce**, or **Robin Reliant**. I know which one I would prefer my Grump to become interested in, but with our budget, a diecast model of Lady Penelope's pink Rolls Royce would be all we could afford.

I'll skip over **reindeer racing** for obvious reasons.

For the brave among you: get him a large tank for keeping **reptiles**. I shared a flat in my youth with a girl who had a chameleon. You never knew where the wretched thing was, and it would drop from the ceiling onto your head without warning. Lucky it wasn't a boa constrictor.

Robot toys, models, and vehicles are always entertaining. If you are cunning, you could get him to build a robot to do the housework.

Blue suede shoes conjure up only one thing for me: **rock and roll**. Whether it is the music, the dancing or the memorabilia from that era, you'll find something to bring out the Teddy Boy in your man.

Rock and Roll originated in the States in the 1950s. It was first encountered by British audiences through films like *Rock Around the Clock* (1955), which featured the Bill Hailey & His Comets hit *Rock Around the Clock*, followed by acts such as Elvis Presley, Little Richard and Buddy Holly.

In 1958, the UK produced its first authentic rock and roll star, Cliff Richard, a man who has maintained his popularity over several decades.

Who was the best 007? Sean Connery, George Lazenby, Roger Moore, Pierce Brosnan, Timothy Dalton, or Daniel Craig? It's a divisive issue that's given rise to endless disputes among film fans. Just who is the best actor to have played James Bond?

Opinions may differ on that subject, but there is no doubt that James Bond appeals to all age groups. There is also large appeal for memorabilia associated with the character, and the actors who have played him.

Roger Moore memorabilia is hugely desirable, and you can even purchase items from Sir Roger Moore's personal website. I expect it is something to do with that eyebrow raising he was so good at, or his gentle humour he brought to the role:

Magda: "He suggests a trade. The egg for your life."

Bond: "Well, I heard the price of eggs was up, but isn't that a little high?"

Octopussy (1983)

A boxed set of all of the *James Bond* films will also keep your cantankerous man quiet for a while.

The most obvious hobby and one that I would happily spend every waking hour doing is **reading**—that is, when I am not enjoying my other favourite hobby: writing.

Whether it is books, magazines, newspapers or the back of cereal packets, your bear has time to indulge himself and read. Good time for him to catch up on all those books you kept buying him for Christmas, which have been on the bookshelf ever since.

To finish this section, let's consider the possibility of **rubber-band powered aircraft**. The Wright Brothers received a simple free-flight rubber-powered aircraft when they were eight and twelve years old. This fuelled their fascination for flight and they eventually embarked on a journey resulting in the invention of man-made flight. Not much scope then for your other half to develop this any further than just a fun hobby.

S

From **sand sculpting** to **synchronised swimming**, with weird and wonderful ideas in between, the letter S offers us a super selection of hobbies and interests for our favourite misery guts.

Okay, sand sculpting isn't going to be a winner, neither is **sand yachting**, nor **sand boarding**, if you live in a town some distance away from the sea, so let's be sensible about it and look at some activities he might be able to have a go at. I'm going to start with one that should at least generate a smile from him when you suggest it: **Scalextrix**.

These model cars and track sets are still hugely popular today. The cars are usually based on real vehicles from Formula 1, Grand Prix, NASCAR, rallying, touring, or Le Mans, or on ordinary road-going cars. Can't you just envisage your other half hiding away in the spare room with his new toy, pretending to be Schumacher or Hamilton?

The longest Scalextrix track was built by James May and a team of volunteers who created a full-length track, closely following the route of the old Brooklands racing track. The event broke the Guinness World Record for the longest ever Scalextrix track in the world, finally measuring 2.95 miles (4.75km).

Who is the only Great Dane in the world to have spots? In dog years, he is 301-years-old. He has a star on Hollywood's Walk of Fame and loves caramel-flavoured snacks. You got it. It's **Scooby Doo**. Technically, his real name is Scoobert "Scooby" Doo, but I am now revealing my true colours here, and yes, I am a fan. Your Grump might also remember the series with fondness, which means you could interest him in some Scooby Doo memorabilia, or at least a set of DVDs to keep him occupied one Saturday morning.

I admit that was a bit of a lame offering, so maybe I can make up for it with this next suggestion. Get your sourpuss involved in **Scrabble**. Challenging and excellent for the memory, this super game can be played on a board, on a phone, online and even on Facebook.

Scrabble is sold in 121 countries and there are 29 different language versions, so you can play Scrabble and practise **Spanish** or **Swedish** at the same time.

Approximately 150 million sets have been sold worldwide. Now that's what I call a triumph (score fifteen or forty-five if played into a triple word space).

The highest possible one-word score in North America is 392. You can achieve this score with only one of five words: OXAZEPAM, BEZIQUES, CAZIQUES, MEZQUITS and MEZQUITE. If only I knew what they all meant.

QUIZZIFY in the English version beats the above words, scoring 410. (Yes, I know there is only one letter Z tile in the English version, but you have a blank tile that you can use as a 'Z' too.)

Let's move away from Scrabble and on to a more active hobby: **scuba diving**. You don't need to send him on a course in the Bahamas for this activity, because there are many Professional Association of Diving Instructors (PADI) courses dotted around the UK, and places to dive.

I learned to scuba dive in my forties at Dosthill, Tamworth, which is the oldest inland dive site in the country. I didn't spot any exotic fish in the quarry, but I was eyeballed by some evil looking pike. I discovered a caravan at about twenty metres and did an emergency ascent that resulted in me looking like the *Creature from the Black Lagoon* with nasty things in my hair and something sticky running down my face.

There seem to be a huge number of retired people who take up this activity. One such example is Brian Wall from Essex, who passed his ocean-diver scuba course at the age of seventy-four, and Burt Kilbride, who was still diving at the age of 93, but has since sadly passed away.

Age does not seem to be a barrier for activities you would

normally attribute to younger people, so purchasing your Grump a wetsuit and fins may not seem as barmy as you first thought.

I am not sure if I should mention this next one, but it certainly conjures up some glorious images in my mind: **stripping**. Please pick yourself off the floor immediately. This could be the hobby you have been searching for.

Bernie Barker from the USA began his career in stripping at the age of sixty as a way to get into shape after recovering from prostate cancer. He left his job as a real estate salesman and became a stripper, winning over forty contests.

If you could get your Grumpy to have a go with some equally grumpy friends, you could even encourage them to do The Full Monty at the annual church Christmas party. Now that would be fun.

Other (more serious) interests beginning with the letter S are **sailing**, **scrap albums**, **sewing**, **shooting**, **shuffleboard**, **skittles**, **snooker**, **stamp collecting**, **Subbuteo**, **Sudoku**, and **swimming**. Slightly different hobbies are **sword swallowing**, **sledge dog racing**, **storm chasing**, **skip diving** (scavenge through skips for discarded items that you may find useful), or any activity that requires you to launch yourself out of an aeroplane, like **skydiving**.

It seems some people need that adrenaline rush even in their twilight years. At 88 years of age, Jim Brierley is the oldest active skydiver in the world. He took part in a tandem sky dive when he was 101 years old.

> "If at first you don't succeed, skydiving is not for you."

Your Grumpy could, of course, become a **steam-train enthusiast**, or even take an interest in **steam traction engines**. There are shows all over the UK, especially from spring onwards. Indulge his interest fully by purchasing a full-sized steam engine and watch his face light up as he crawls down the high street on it.

Having an interest in the **stock market** has its highs and lows (much like the market itself). I am always reminded of the joke: "How do you make a small fortune on the Stock Markets?" "Start with a big one!" This is, however a time-consuming interest that should keep your Grumpy glued to every financial programme on television and online most of the day. Your phone bill will increase as he makes his daily call to the stock broker to be reassured that his fortune is really not withering away. Be patient with him. He'll need your understanding with this one.

So, as we come to the end of choices for hobbies beginning with the letter S, I'll leave you with another short list. You might just discover a "possible" in it: **Star Trek, sea shell collecting, sheep dog trials, snuff boxes, softball, stencilling, stone skimming,** and **spiritual healing.**

T

Titillate and tantalise your man with one or more of these tempting ideas.

Introduce him to tweeting by starting up a **Twitter** account for him. I didn't "get" Twitter to start with. However, I am now a convert. I have a stream from Hootsuite showing me the latest tweets as I type my novels. I love to know what is going on in the world and what is #trending. I am not alone. It's simple to use, and you only need to use 140 characters per message, called a tweet, which is ideal for a taciturn grump.

Twitter currently has approximately 500 million users and one of them, Ivy Bean, began tweeting at the grand old age of one hundred and three from her residential home in the outskirts of Bradford. She became an internet sensation through Facebook, but switched to Twitter in 2009. She amassed over 56,000 followers with posts about food, family visits and even an invitation from Gordon Brown to meet the then prime minister. She wrote over 1,000 tweets, documenting several episodes of *Deal or No Deal,* her favourite food—fish and chip dinners—and a friendship with the singer Peter Andre.

My own grouch hates the modern word and is bewildered by technology. He would be the last person on the planet to have a smartphone, let alone a Twitter account. Technology makes him even more cantankerous than usual. He is happier with the world the way it used to be, when there was no internet.

He feels the same way about television. He constantly complains about the rubbish on "the box". We seem to spend all our time watching repeats of television shows from the seventies.

For a grouchy man who prefers television, and life, "the way it was", purchase a DVD set of his favourite childhood programmes like **Tintin, Thunderbirds,** or **Thomas the Tank Engine**. Should this be of interest, he could take it further and join the thousands of people who collect memorabilia connected to these characters and shows.

It has been proven that people who own an animal are more content than those who don't. You don't have to nip down to the local kennels, though, to buy your Grump a canine friend. Get him a **Tamagotchi**. They are back in fashion again.

These are small virtual "pets" that you nurture until they are "fully grown". Like a real pet, they require feeding, playing with and looking after. Clearly, they are much cheaper than the real thing, yet you must make sure you do your job, or your virtual pet will turn into a little monster.

During the eighties, I ended up looking after my son's Tamagotchi while he was at school. I had to keep remembering to sort it out and walk it and so on—difficult, since I was at work at the time.

Sports beginning with the letter T include **tennis, table tennis, Taekwon-Do, target shooting, ten pin bowling, tiddlywinks, trampolining,** or the curious sport of **toe wrestling**. Although you wouldn't want him to try it out on you, he can go along to a pub where they perform this strange activity.

It was devised in the 1970s by George Burgess, because he wanted to give England the chance to be world-beaters in at least one sporting sphere. Dreams were shattered though, when a visiting Canadian won the inaugural event. Since then, it has grown in popularity. Competitors have to wrestle each other using only their big toes in a knockout competition.

World championships are held at the Bentley Brook Inn in Derbyshire, and in 2012 were won by Alan "Nasty" Nash, who regained the title in a brutal bout. Not to be performed if your toenails are long.

Bring out the cultural side of your Grumpy by introducing him to the **theatre**. Surely there must be something on that he would enjoy. It doesn't have to be a Shakespearian play. You could take him to a musical; start with *Grumpy Old Men*, the musical.

For daytime amusement, buy him some shears, and leave him in the garden shaping the Buxus semperviens into a large teapot or swan. The art of sculpting ornamental bushes in gardens goes back to the imaginative creations in ancient Egyptian and Roman gardens, and blossomed during the Renaissance, where clipped alleys and avenues were an important part of the cultural scene. Today, with easy access to frames and materials, anyone, even a Grumpy, can create **topiary**. Supervise him in case his creative urges take over. You don't want to go outside and discover you have a giant hamburger.

According to the website www.taxidermyhobbist.com, "**taxidermy** is a fun and fascinating hobby". If your man is a hunter, he'll no doubt want to show off his trophies, and taxidermy is one way to ensure he'll have a memento of his kills. For artists, it is becoming an avant-garde addition to many other visual disciplines. Think Damien Hurst and formaldehyde. Glassy-eyed stuffed animals don't do it for me, but as long as he stays away from Tiddles the cat and is happy, I'll put up with anything.

Every man is a small boy at heart when it comes to **trains**. We covered this topic under the letter S too. Refrain from calling him the "Fat Controller".

My son recently came home wearing one of these on his head: a **traffic cone**. Apparently, it was in a field, so he procured it. For a reason I can't explain, men seem to like collecting cones. This in itself seems odd, because whenever we are travelling on a motorway, my Grump complains nonstop about the number of cones blocking the outside lane.

It is not advisable to go around stealing traffic cones, as this could put others at risk, but you can collect them.

David Morgan, who rather conveniently is sales director of the plastics factory that is the world's largest producer of cones, has the biggest collection of traffic cones in England.

He began collecting them in 1986, and set the Guinness World Record with 137 different traffic cones. Since that record, his collection has grown to over 550 different cones. He keeps them in a lock-up where no harmful UV light might break down the plastic.

As far as cones go, I would rather collect the ones that hold ice cream.

Did you know that **tropical fish** tanks have been known to reduce stress, tension, and anxiety? When humans are relaxed, stress levels drop. Restaurants, doctors' surgeries, offices, hospitals, and hotels are just a few places that typically house a tropical fish tank in their waiting room or lobby. Watching fish swim around in the aquarium relaxes you. Not only does the sound of running water from the aquarium have a soothing effect on you, but the peaceful movements of the fish as they move effortlessly through the water also have a relaxing effect on humans. When we are relaxed, we tend not to complain so much. What are you waiting for? Sit Grumpy Guts in front of a goldfish bowl or an aquarium on a regular basis, and watch him calm down and cheer up.

In a similar vein, cultivating or nurturing **tropical plants** directly improves health and productivity in humans. Fatigue, headaches, coughing and irritated eyes can be cut by having tropical plants in your home or garden. Many offices have tropical plants to help lessen stress levels in their employees and improve general health.

It is possible to recreate an environment to grow plants at home you would normally associate with warmer climates. Your man needs to research their natural environment before he buys, because some plants might require special attention over winter. With careful planning, you could find yourself looking out on palm and banana trees and your Grumpy dressed in a sarong.

Treasure hunting[6] is not your usual hobby, but a retired Grumpy has oodles of time on his hands, so he may as well do something that offers more than just passing time.

He can go on treasure-hunting holidays. In the United States, the Crater of Diamonds State Park in Arkansas is the only place on earth that allows visitors to dig for diamonds. You can rent all the digging and mining equipment you will need at the park. There isn't even any restriction on how much "treasure" a visitor is allowed to carry with him either. If your little Pirate of the Caribbean is fortunate enough to find a sparkly diamond the size of the Koh-i-Noor, he can bring it home for you. Well, he would want you to have it, wouldn't he?

Send him to Cherokee Ruby Mine in Franklin, Carolina, for rubies; the Emerald Hollow Mine, Hiddenite, Carolina, for emeralds; the Gem Mountain Sapphire Mine, Philipsburg, Montana, for those pretty blue sapphires; the Spruce Pine Aqua Marine Mine, Spruce Pine, North Carolina for sparkling aqua marine stones or even the Roaring Camp Gold Mine, Pine Grove, California, to ensure he has a chance of returning home with some decent gems and gold for your jewellery collection.

Final suggestions to finish off this chapter are **toy forts, trucks**, and **tango dancing**.

question: what sort of music do cows
like to tango to?
answer: any kind of "moosic".

6   Read more at Buzzle: http://www.buzzle.com/articles/treasure-hunting-vacation-where-to-go.html

U

Although there are a few activities beginning with the letter U, I'm guessing they will be unlikely choices for your Grump. Still, unusual hobbies might be just what your unique man is looking for, so what about introducing him to **UFOs** or **urban chicken-keeping**?

Most people will have seen a **unicycle** at a circus or parade, where they are one of the stock items used by clowns. Unicycles were believed to have been inspired by the penny-farthing. They first became popular towards the end of the 1960s, but now, unicycling has developed into different forms of competition, such as **unicycle hockey** or **unicycle basketball**.

In recent years, **extreme unicycling** has seen increased growth around the world, particularly Canada. Athletes can often be found jumping sets of steps or grinding handrails, which are techniques often used by skateboarders.

One such accomplished and skilled extreme unicyclist is Terry "Unigeezer" Peterson, born January 15th, 1956. An inspiration for many men over the age of fifty, Terry first learned to ride a unicycle at the age of ten. He gave it up for four decades and started to ride it again at the age of fifty. Since then, he has accomplished some incredible achievements, including climbing the famous Fargo Street's massive thirty-three percent grade at the annual event in the Silverlake district of Los Angeles in 2011. Not satisfied with doing it once, he did it twice. He has also ridden a 36-inch unicycle 104 miles in one day for the American Cancer Society charity. He has been a subject of a documentary about extreme unicycling, featured in a book and on a national commercial for Ford Fiesta.

With groups, clubs and associations worldwide, this is far more popular than you might imagine. Add three soft balls to it, and your man could take up **unicycle juggling**.

unicycle definitions:
unisex: how baby unicycles are made.
unicorn: maize eaten while riding.

Please also let me point out that Coldplay produced a video of an elephant riding a **unicycle** for their single Paradise, and in my opinion, Coldplay are "cool", which makes unicycling cool.

I'm abandoning the idea of talking about **UFOs**, since many grumpy old men are sceptics and won't believe in aliens. Consequently, my next choice is **urban-exploring**. This is historically done in natural caves, but has gained popularity among some town and city dwellers.

Urban-exploring involves going into areas and buildings not normally open to the public, like old ruined hospitals, churches, tunnels and other places of historical interest. Of course, your Grumpy will be committing trespass to do this, so it is only advisable if you don't mind him spending time at the local police station.

Ensure he gets permission from the relevant authorities first. Urban explorers attempt to look after the places they visit. They value the history, document it and take photographs.

There are quite a few websites, forums and groups, should he settle on this pastime and require further information. You'll know he's decided on this hobby when he sneaks off wearing dark clothes and a furtive look on his face.

Urban chicken-keeping is a fast-growing hobby in the UK. Modern compact chicken houses can be purchased to keep your chickens safe from the rapidly increasing population of urban foxes; I wonder if there is a connection there? You must make sure your chickens are vaccinated, and have fresh food and water. That's all you need to ensure a supply of eggs and, of course, Christmas dinner.

question: why did the chicken cross the road, roll in the mud, and cross the road again?
answer: because he was a dirty double-crosser.

question: why did the turkey cross the road?
answer: to prove he wasn't chicken.

Do you remember Lord Charles or Nooky the Bear? How could you forget the haunting song, *I Wish I Could Fly* by Orville the Duck? Of course, all these have something in common: they are all **ventriloquists'** puppets.

My first memory of ventriloquism was seeing a woman called Shari Lewis talking to a sock, which was named Lamb Chop. From that moment, I wanted to be a ventriloquist and practised "Gottle of Geer" for months.

Find an old sock and introduce your GOM to this inexpensive hobby. If nothing else, he would have someone else to moan to for a while.

Being a Grump, he'll always complain about the cost of your weekly shop. Encourage him to start a **vegetable garden** to help bring down your expenditure. He'll be content at the thought of how much he is saving, and will be very busy preparing the ground, sowing seed, fighting with slugs and nurturing his crops. Of course, you could just have a virtual garden like those you can tend on Facebook. They are less expensive and equally time-consuming.

Let your man take **videos**. No, not those sorts of videos! With all the new technology available, it is becoming easier to make videos. You can get a simple and not-too-costly camera, which can take videos in slow motion or black and white and so on. He could amuse himself making a short film, or just take nice videos of your children and grandchildren blowing out the candles on their birthday cake.

Does your man like a little tipple of wine? Take it one step further and buy him a **vineyard**. Well, not quite an entire vineyard, just a line of vines in a vineyard. More and more vineyards are allowing you to sponsor vines. You get a certificate, an invite to the chateau or vineyard to see your vines and, at the end of a year, get to sample or purchase wine from your vines.

Some vineyards run courses on how to make wine, or you can join the harvest and collect the grapes from your own vines.

Once he gets into this hobby, check out vineyards for sale in France, Portugal or even New Zealand. It could be the beginning of a whole new life.

One of the oldest clubs for enthusiasts is the **VW Volkswagen (GB) Club**. VW cars, famously known as 'Beetles', or 'Bugs', have been incredibly popular since they were first launched in 1938. The Herbie films, beginning with *The Love Bug* in 1968, popularised them further, and today there are numerous clubs and events throughout the UK and world. Take, for example, the annual Bug Jam Event held at the Santa Pod racetrack, which is often dubbed 'Glastonbury On Wheels' and which offers a host of activities for an enthusiast. An interest guaranteed to put a smile on his face.

question: how many elephants can you fit into a vw beetle?
answer: four. two in the front and two in the back.

question: how can you tell if there is an elephant in the fridge?
answer: footprints in the butter.

question: how can you tell if there are two elephants in the fridge?
answer: two sets of footprints in the butter and the food keeps disappearing.

question: how can you tell if there
are three elephants in the fridge?
answer: you can't close the fridge
door.

question: how can you tell if there
are four elephants in the fridge?
answer: there's a vw beetle in the
driveway.

I was going to remark that, unless you live by a beach, I think **volleyball** is a hobby that might not have much appeal for you, and yet, during my research, I discovered that is not the case, since volleyball is the second most popular sport in the world after football. I was clearly thinking about beach volleyball, which is different.

Volleyball was originally called "mintonette" and invented in 1895 by William G. Morgan. Beach volleyball, however, didn't get played until 1930.

It became an Olympic sport in 1964 and is played by men and women. A volleyball player jumps approximately three hundred times during a match. Again, this isn't just a sport for young people. There are tournaments and clubs for seniors, so, no excuse for your gloomy chap, who could take up this sport at his local health club or recreation centre.

If you are still struggling to find an interest even at this stage of the book, then this next one must be the right one for your Grump. It is almost like sending him back to work and will make him feel appreciated and useful: **volunteering**.

There are so many possibilities in this category, I could write another book about them. Get your GOM to check out volunteering choices from his local volunteer centre or local library. It might be advisable for you to go with him to give him some direction, and also to prevent him from walking out in a funk when he is directed to a huge section in the library to look up the choices in a very large book.

It is best if he chooses something that can use the skills he has amassed over his working life, so for example, if he is good at maths, get him to tutor someone who needs help. If he has knowledge of the building industry, he could volunteer for some community projects that can use those skills.

There is a vast array of possibilities, including canal clearing, working in hospices or helping animals. You can sign up to work as a volunteer for the National Trust, in care homes, hospitals, for sanctuaries or even to work in schools as an assistant. Some even give you a uniform, or pay your travelling costs. Now, that should make him happier.

Other hobbies include **vacuum cleaners**—actually, I'm all for that one if it means he'll do the hoovering every other day—**Victorian Staffordshire pottery**, **veterans' rugby**, **vintage cars**, **vintage vans**, **vintage lorries** and **vintage buses**, **vintage farm machinery**, **vintage luggage**, **virtual model railways**, or becoming a **virtual pilot**. I wonder if you could join in and become a virtual passenger and sit in virtual first class with a virtual glass of virtual champagne—virtually impossible, I would guess.

There is plenty of variety among these hobbies and activities for your grouch. I hope you find one at least to give him some variation in his day and keep him from **vegetating**.

We have been weaving our way through many wild ideas and possibilities, but now we arrive at another wacky one with **welly throwing**. Welly throwing is often to be found at fêtes, and involves throwing a wellington boot the furthest distance. It may sound simple enough, but technique is paramount to a good throw, and you require good coordination with a firm grip of the boot to ensure a lengthy throw. Get the crabby one to practise by throwing his wellies at the cat, who spends all night yowling on your garden fence. He'll enjoy that.

My son was heavily into **Warhammer**, which is far more than just assembling and meticulously painting small armies of weird monsters, forming battalions, and leaving small tubs of paint all over the house and carpet. It is another fantasy game, which can be acted out with fellow Warhammer enthusiasts.

Games and tutorials are held in Games Workshop shops, where you often see men and boys huddled over tiny figures, painting intricate details on them.

It enjoys considerable worldwide popularity, and Warhammer manuals and stories based on Warhammer characters can be purchased from all good outlets. In 2011, a Warhammer film entitled *Ultramarines: A Warhammer 40,000 Movie* was released.

I have several large boxes of unused and unpainted figures along with numerous pots and spray cans of paint, should you require them. They are currently cluttering up my wardrobes in the spare room, so please take them off my hands.

If you managed to get your little David Bailey Grump interested in photography, take it one step further and suggest he begins taking **wedding photographs**. He could earn some money from this hobby. On second thoughts, Grumpies are naturally programmed to grimace, and that demeanour wouldn't be appropriate for the occasion.

I shall now waft past **weaving**, **Wedgewood porcelain**,

white-knuckle rides, Wild West re-enactment, and **whale watching** and whip onto **water divining,** also known as dowsing.

For most people, a mention of water divining conjures up a man walking across fields with a tree branch trying to find underground water. This art has been with us for thousands of years and is used for more than just seeking out water. Dowsing has also been used to find missing objects and people, for healing, food allergy testing and to discover the siting of ley lines and energy centres.

Although there is no firm scientific evidence to prove it is right, dowsers are regularly used by the police and the armed forces, while major oil companies have also employed dowsers rather than move highly expensive, highly technical equipment around.

Whether you chose a pendulum, a Y stick or L rods, the technique must be practised regularly. It might be the hobby for him, especially if he cracks it and discovers an oil field in the back garden.

There are some wild sporting activities that can be taken up by an adventurous Grump. Look at **water polo, water skiing,** or **wakeboarding.** Wakeboarders are towed behind a speedboat, much like a water skier, except he/she only uses a single board. The wakeboarder attempts various jumps and other tricks, unless he is useless at this sport, in which case he falls off the board and has to be picked up by the speedboat.

Collectible items beginning with the letter W include **watches, Wade porcelain, walking sticks, wall plaques, Wallace and Gromit items,** and **wine.** I must pause here to emit a sigh of contentment.

Wine is a fascinating hobby, and I don't just mean swigging back bottles of Chardonnay. I have already touched upon the possibility of owning part of a vineyard, yet collecting wine is equally absorbing. There is plenty of information available from websites, magazines, clubs and associations. You can even drop by your local wine store to sample wines and decide upon a few bottles for your new wine cellar, or in our case, wine rack.

Some activities you would normally associate with younger people have been embraced by the older generation. Otto Comanos, who was born on 16th November 1913 in Greece, took up **windsurfing** upon his retirement in 1986. He now windsurfs two or three times a week in and around the lakes of Sydney, New South Wales, Australia, and holds the Guinness Book of Records (2013) record for being the world's oldest windsurfer.

Not for the faint-hearted, but daredevil pensioner Thomas Lackey from Gloucestershire began **wingwalking** at the age of 82 after his wife, Isabel, passed away. Rather poignantly, he carries a photograph of her on every flight.

Born 22nd May 1920, Mr Lackey became the world's oldest wingwalker a few years ago, but smashed his own record in May 2012, when he got his 27th wingwalk under his belt. What are you waiting for? Make sure your grumpy guts is wearing a warm vest, and "Chocks away!"

For those who prefer the comfort of their homes, you might suggest **woodcarving**, **whittling**, **wire sculpting**, or of course, **writing**.

I am clearly prejudiced, but I think writing is a fabulous hobby. You don't have to write novels or entertaining books. You can settle for short stories, flash fiction, poetry and so on. There are competitions galore online, and so many websites for authors I cannot begin to list them all. I shall mention one of the websites I write for because it would be churlish not to: Indies Unlimited, which offers advice, tutorials and support to all budding authors.

You don't have to be reliant on your computer, because there are creative writing classes scattered throughout the country. Your Grumpy can find like-minded people at all of them, who are willing to help him begin a career in writing.

QUESTION: HOW MANY MYSTERY WRITERS
DOES IT TAKE TO CHANGE A LIGHT BULB?
ANSWER: TWO. ONE TO SCREW IT ALMOST
ALL THE WAY IN, AND THE OTHER TO GIVE
IT A SURPRISING TWIST AT THE END.

Failing that, you could suggest he takes an interest in **word games**, then amuse yourself listening to all the words he can muster up to protest against this particular hobby.

Other options include painting with **watercolours, watching birds** and then maybe painting them with watercolours, or just **walking**. We covered that in an earlier chapter, but it is worth mentioning again because of the benefits it offers. He could even take his watercolours, in case he gets the urge to paint while out.

For Grumpies who are interested in technology and want to mess about on the internet, he can start a new hobby and turn it into a small business by becoming a **web designer**. He could even use those watercolours he has been painting with to make nice headers and backgrounds for new customers.

I was listening to melodic sounds accompanying the radio last night. It was coming from Mr G as he scrabbled about in the fridge looking for a bar of chocolate to eat. He was **whistling**; rather tunefully as it happens. I checked today, and indeed, whistling is a hobby. I think I might get some Roger Whittaker CDs for him, and shut him in a room to perfect his pitch.

There are several types of whistling techniques, including pucker whistling. This is where you purse your lips—the most common form of whistling, used in melodic whistling. Finger whistling or wolf whistling, employed by builders all over the country when they see a young lady pass by, is where you insert fingers to shape the opening in the mouth. Palatal or roof whistling uses the tongue and roof of the mouth. Hand Whistling is where you cup your hands in front of your face and blow into the chamber to make it resonate. Bottom-lip whistling is performed by sucking air into the mouth, and turbulence is created by pinching the bottom lip at the centre. Teeth whistling and throat whistling are two other choices.

Here's a wild card: **wild-game hunting**. I don't expect you to pack him off with a twelve-bore shotgun to go and hunt down leopards. Just take him on a safari with his camera, and maybe his watercolours. Hunting for the big five is one of the greatest thrills you can have. It's a costly trip if you take him to South Africa, but well worth it. Going back through and admiring the photographs and videos he took will also take up considerable time. Should South Africa be out of your budget, then I am afraid you'll have to settle for a local safari park. Don't let him go alone. The last time I took my own Grumpy to one, he had a standoff with a monkey and had to be rescued before things turned nasty.

All grumpy old men complain about the weather, so why not invest in a **weather station**? That way, he'll know that it is going to pour down, and be able to start complaining in advance.

Weather stations are accurate and fun. We have one. Actually, we have three in case one decided to be optimistic and shows us a brighter day ahead. Your little Michael Fish-a-like will be able to find out not only about the temperature and potential for the day, but also about the wind speed and moon phases. He can then compare his forecast to the one given by the weather forecasters on television, and feel superior when his turns out to be more accurate.

My last offering in this chapter is one that will solve all problems. Your Grumpy will be out of your hair, and you'll be able to carry on as normal. Send him back to **work**.

XYZ

Apart from introducing Grump to **Xena Warrior Princess** or the **X-Files**, there is not much I can recommend in this category. **Xylophone-playing** is the only other possibility I can conjure up.

Letter Y doesn't have a great deal more to offer than letter X, but he could try **yachting**, playing with **yo-yos**, or **Yorkshire pudding racing**. The latter takes place in Brawby, North Yorkshire, and was dreamed up by Simon Thackray in the early 1990s as he stared out of a window at his local pub one sunny Sunday afternoon.

Large Yorkshire puddings are made in the traditional way with flour, eggs and water— although stronger bread flour replaces the normal flour used in this dish—and are cooked and strengthened on the inside with wire. The outside is coated in varnish, to help repel water leakage.

The Yorkshire Pudding Boat Race® attracts much media attention each year. The races are usually undertaken by children, who are lighter than adults, but we all know that Grumpies are children at heart and would love to leap in and have a go. If this doesn't float his (Yorkshire-pudding) boat, he could just learn how to cook them, and save you the hassle every Sunday.

Yodelling may not seem the likeliest of hobbies, but believe me when I tell you it is still taken up by people today. I discovered an eleven-year-old yodelling sensation on YouTube while searching out hobbies for grumpy old men.

The verb "to yodel" comes from the German "jodeln" with the meaning "to utter the syllable jo" (which is pronounced "yo" in German).

You might have heard of Jack Guthrie, who was known as "Oklahoma's Yodeling Cowboy". I hadn't. However, when I asked Mr G if he had heard of him, he burst into song, so there is a chance your own man might also know of Guthrie, even though he was famous in the thirties and early forties.

One of the most famous yodelling songs is *The Lion Sleeps Tonight* also known as *Wimoweh*. Bet you're already singing it. It was first recorded in South African by Solomon Linda and the Evening Birds in 1939, and has since been covered several times over the last few decades.

All together now "In the jungle, the mighty jungle..."

Of course, there is always **yoga**. A hobby guaranteed to make your man supple and relaxed. It is very good for the mind too, and its calming influence thanks to concentrating on the movements will have huge benefits for your grumpy old man. That is, if you can convince him standing on one leg with a whole bunch of women is a good idea.

It is, on a serious note, a very popular hobby. A male who practices yoga is called a yogi or yogin. A female who practices is called a yogini. Once more, age is not a barrier, and in early 2012, 93-year-old Tao Porchon Lynch was declared the world's oldest yoga teacher.

See if you can convince your Grump to change his ways and take it up.

In yoga, it's just one thing after another~breath, breath, breath.

Sadly, we come towards the end of the book with the letter Z, but what an end! Your Grump could try out **Zen meditation**.

If he is more energetic, you could try to treat him to classes in **Zumba**. There will be mostly women attending, and his rhythm will undoubtedly be dreadful, so this is clutching at straws, yet he would not be alone if he takes up this hobby.

Mr Edward Clarke, a retired baker born in Wrexham, believes more men should be encouraged to join fitness classes. Aged ninety-six, he is mastering Zumba, the Latin dance-inspired fitness program, which was created in Colombia and has become a fitness craze. Mr Clarke, who has been a keen dancer all his life, is the oldest and only male member of the weekly Zumba Gold over-50s dance club that meets every Thursday. His philosophy about life and his hobby is sensible: "Time is valuable. Use it."

If you have really had enough of your Grumpy, and no other idea in this book appeals whatsoever, then look to **zorbing**. This is essentially rolling down a hill in a plastic ball. You'll probably have to dupe him into it a bit, but just think of the pleasure you'll get when you push him off and watch him roll down a hill, like a giant hamster in a ball, yelling loudly as he goes.

I hope you have found a few ideas here to keep your curmudgeon out of your hair for a while. Better still, I hope he now has an activity that will make him forget he is a GOM and remind him that life is for living, whatever your age.

If he still can't decide what to do and is hanging about grumbling, then I suggest you take up one of these hobbies and leave him to get on with it. Good luck!

Following the successful publication of her first two novels
Mini Skirts and Laughter Lines
Surfing in Stilettos

readers emailed for advice on what to do with a retired
grumpy old man like the character of Phil in those books.

Two Non Fiction books followed:
How Not to Murder your Grumpy
Grumpy Old Menopause

Also by Carol E. Wyer:
Novels:
Just Add Spice
Three Little Birds
Life Swap
Non Fiction:
Grumpies on Board
Short stories: *Love Hurts*
Carol is a member of the RNA (Romantic Novelists Association).

Mini Skirts and Laughter Lines

Amanda Wilson can't decide between murder, insanity, or another glass of
red wine. Facing fifty and all that it entails is problematic enough. What's
the point in minking your eyes when your husband would rather watch
Russia Today than admire you strutting in front of the television in only
thigh boots and a thong?
Her son has managed to perform yet another magical disappearing act.
Could he actually be buried under the mountain of festering washing
strewn on his bedroom floor? He'll certainly be buried somewhere when
she next gets her hands on him.
At least her mother knows how to enjoy herself. She's partying her twilight
years away in Cyprus. Queen of the Twister mat, she now has a toy boy in
tow.
Amanda knows she shouldn't have pressed that Send, button. The past
always catches up with you sooner or later. Still, her colourful past is a
welcome relief to her monochrome present—especially when it comes in
the shape of provocative Todd Bradshaw, her first true love.
Amanda has a difficult decision to make – one that will require more than a
few glasses of Chianti.

Just Add Spice

Dawn Ellis needs to escape from her painfully dull existence. Her unemployed husband spends all day complaining about life, moping around, or fixing lawnmowers on her kitchen table. The local writing class proves to be an adequate distraction with its eccentric collection of wannabe authors and, of course, the enigmatic Jason, who soon shows a romantic interest in her.

Dawn pours her inner frustrations into her first novel about the extraordinary exploits of Cinnamon Knight, an avenging angel -- a woman who doesn't believe in following the rules. Cinnamon is ruthless and wanton, inflicting suffering on any man who warrants it. Little does Dawn realise that soon the line between reality and fiction will blur. Her own life will be transformed, and those close to her will pay the price.

Surfing in Stilettos

Amanda Wilson is all geared up for an exciting gap-year, travelling across Europe. She soon finds her plans thwarted when she is abandoned in France with only a cellarful of Chateau Plonk, a large, orange Space Hopper, and Old Ted, the dog, for company.

Fate has intervened to turn Amanda's life on its head. First, Bertie, the camper van, breaks down. Then her dopey son, Tom, who is staying in their house in the UK, is wrecking it, one piece at a time. Next, the jaw-dropping video Skype calls that her irrepressible mother insists on making are, by contrast, making Amanda's humdrum trip even less palatable.

Finally, she discovers that her new-found, French friend, Bibi Chevalier, had engineered a plan to ensure that her philandering husband would never stray again; unfortunately, Amanda is unwittingly drawn into the scheme, becoming a target.

Meanwhile, on a beach in Sydney, a lonely Todd Bradshaw realises that his first true love, Amanda Wilson, is definitely the only woman for him. Can he get back into her good books and hopefully back into her arms with his latest plan? Or will fate intervene yet again and turn everyone's lives upside down?

Grumpy old Menopause

Have you started to write post-it notes with your kids' names on them? Do you need to change your underwear after every sneeze? Guess it's time to read this book then. It'll help you get through "that" time in your life with a spring in your step and a smile on your face. With numerous suggestions, sensible advice and amusing anecdotes, Grumpy Old Menopause will help you sail through that tricky part of a woman's life with ease and humour. It should prevent you from turning into Mrs Crabby or worse still, a demonic monster.

"An excellent mix of humour and sound advice. This book is a must-read for all women ... I highly recommend Grumpy Old Menopause. It is the perfect blend of humour and excellent advice to help all women sail through the menopause." - Nicky Snazell, Fi STOP Consultant Physiotherapist in Spinal Pain, Fellow of Institute for the Study and Treatment of Pain. International Lecturer in Pain and Health

JUST ADD SPICE

"Written with the sassy humour, clever plot and laugh a minute honesty we come to expect from Carol E Wyer." – Bookish Bits

"This book is so worth gushing about – I adored it. Carol Wyer sure knows how to make people laugh." – Chicklit Pad

LIFE SWAP

"A novel infused with warm humour." British Comedy Guide

GRUMPY OLD MENOPAUSE

"If Robin Williams were a woman chronicling the changes of Menopause, he'd be Carol Wyer. Screamingly funny, seemingly hypomanic, and ultimately upbeat, she casts her comedic eye on the Change from A to Z." – The Menopause Goddess

HOW NOT TO MURDER YOUR GRUMPY

"Entertaining book with good advice" – Simon Mayo presenter BBC Radio 2

"I recommend it to all men and women over 40 and appreciate the author's pledge that "No grumpy old men were harmed in the writing of this book." – Jed Diamond Ph.D., author and Irritable Male Syndrome expert.

"I'd recommend this to both men and women of all ages – it will give you a good belly laugh." The Daily Opinion